SKETCHES

OF THE PIONEERS IN BURKE COUNTY HISTORY

By Col. Thomas George Walton

⍦

Being Reminiscenses and Sketches, prepared by the late Colonel T. G. Walton for the old Morganton Herald. A Rich Fund of Historical Incidents Connected with the Early Settlers of Western North Carolina

(The articles comprising the first section of this book, pages 5 through 67, were written in 1894, and published in the old Morganton Herald. They were reprinted in the Herald in 1924, beginning April 10, and were found in the papers of Elisa M. Pearson. Those from pages 68 through 89 were copied from manuscripts of Col. Walton now in the possession of his granddaughter, Mrs. Harry Boggs).

(Grateful appreciation is extended to The News-Herald Publishing Co. for the use of plates for approximately 50 pages of this collection).

Originally Published 1894
By: Col. Thomas George Walton

New Material Copyright: 2016
Southern Historical Press, Inc.

Please direct all correspondence and orders to:

www.southernhistoricalpress.com
or
SOUTHERN HISTORICAL PRESS, Inc.
PO BOX 1267
375 West Broad Street
Greenville, SC   29601
southernhistoricalpress@gmail.com

ISBN #0-89308-538-3

Printed in the United States of America

THOMAS GEORGE WALTON — 1815-1905

FOREWORD

Beginning Jan. 11, 1894 the Morganton Herald (now the News-Herald) published at least 15 papers by Col. T. Geo. Walton under the title "Sketches of the Pioneers in Burke County History," most of which are given in this booklet. It seems fitting to say something of this remarkable man, who died in 1905 when nearly 90 years old. (As far as is known he wrote nothing of the Walton family.)

George Walton, the great-grandfather of Col. Walton, emigrated to this country in 1682, and his son, Thomas Walton, came to Burke County from Amherst County, Virginia, before 1803. Little is known of Col. Walton's early life. He was born Oct. 5, 1815 in the home of his father on the northeast corner of Union and Greene streets, Morganton, opposite the Gov. Caldwell home (now the site of the Caldwell Hotel.) The house where he was born is said to have been built by his father in 1810, and was later known as Hotel Morgan. From this house his father conducted the business of Postmaster. (He served two terms, the first in 1803, Morganton's second postmaster.)

It is probable that Col. Walton had tutors, according to the custom of that day. He had a large library of calf-bound books, and was an omniverous reader to the end of his days. He was brought up a Presbyterian and probably attended that church from 1830 until 1846, when the first Episcopal Church in Morganton was built.

These papers of Col. Walton were so enjoyed by Burke citizens that the Herald reprinted 11 of them in 1924 (four sets now extant); and some of the earlier printing had been lost when files of the paper were destroyed. At the time of Col. Walton's death, Col. W. S. Pearson wrote an appreciation of him in which it was stated that he was an earnest Whig in ante-bellum days, and a staunch Republican after Reconstruction. Son of a prominent merchant, he was a large slave-holder, and owned valuable real estate in Burke County. A devoted Episcopalian he was a vestryman of Grace Church, Morganton, for 50 years. He married Eliza Murphy (daughter of John Murphy and Margaret Avery) on Dec. 28, 1837 at "Willow Hill," which house is still standing near Canoe Creek.

Col. Walton was a gentleman farmer and represented Burke in the House of Commons in 1850. He was a director of the State Hospital in Raleigh, and one of the original directors of the State Hospital in Morganton. Being 46 years old at the beginning of the Civil War, he was made a colonel in charge of reserves in Burke. He was stationed at Camp Wyatt, N. C., in 1862 and at Fort Fisher near Wilmington, in 1863, as shown by his letters.

He built "Creekside" in about 1836, adjoining a house built by the Greenlees in 1800, both parts still standing. He and his wife were the parents of 11 children born in this house (now the home of his granddaughter, Mrs. Harry Boggs). Three sons served in the Confederate Army. He was the fifth Walton of the name in this country, being the great-nephew of George Walton who signed the Declaration of Independence.

"Should auld acquaintance be forgot,

And never bro't to min'?

Should auld acquaintance be forgot,

And days o' auld lang syne?"

Having recently been in the habit of speaking of scenes, occurrences and anecdotes, characteristic and illustrative, of the early settlers of Burke County, as well as of persons contemporaneous with myself, many of whom have gone to that "bourne from whence no traveler returns", at the request of a number of the citizens of the county I have concluded to jot down, in a desultory way, reminiscences of the past in connection with some of our leading citizens and others. The author of "The Seasons" said, "Old age becomes garrulous." As the writer has passed by some years the age allotted to man, I may not be an exception; however this may be, I will set down naught in malice.

My first recollection of Morganton and its environs was at the age of three years, in the month of December, 1819, when my brother, Wm. M. [McEntire] Walton, was born. At that time my father, Thomas Walton, was living in a house in which he was merchandising, at the intersection of Union and Green streets. I remember distinctly the crying of the babe. There was snow upon the ground, and my two elder brothers, James and John, were engaged in catching snowbirds under a dead-fall in the garden. My long tried and beloved friend, the late Gov. [T.R.] Caldwell [1818] (born about two years after I was, in the same town) and myself, speaking of our first recollections, in proof of my wonderfully tenacious memory in having related this incident, replied: "Why, Tom, I can beat that all hollow; I was at Cherry Fields a short time since, talking with my mother about how lasting impressions were made in early life. I remembered distinctly the death of a child of Major [Jacob of Cedar Grove] Forney's, caused by falling on a pair of pointed scissors. She responded, "Well done, Tod; you have the most remarkable memory of anyone I ever knew, for that happened ten years before you were born!" So, my readers of these reminiscences will note the possibility of my making the same mistake in some of the incidents spoken of as did my friend.

Burke county was erected out of a part of Rowan county at a General Assembly held at Newbern on the 8th day of April, 1777, Richard Caswell being Governor, and Samuel Ashe, Speaker of the Senate; Abner Nash was Speaker of the Commons. Beginning at the Catawba river on the line between Rowan and Tryon counties thence running up the meanders of said river to the north end of an island known as the three-cornered island; thence north to the ridge that divides the Yadkin and Catawba waters; then westerly along the ridge to the mountain known as the Blue Mountain[1],—which divides the eastern and western waters; covering all that portion of Rowan that lies west and south of said line,—covering a large territory from which, from time to time, had been erected many other counties.

Morgan district was made up of the counties of Burke, Wilkes, Rutherford, Lincoln, Washington, and Sullivan. The Superior Court of this district was held twice a year at the court house in Morganton, and in 1788 Col. Sevier, one of the Kings Mountain heroes, was brought here a prisoner and arraigned under a charge of treason, for attempting to form a state out of North Carolina territory west of the Blue Ridge, under the name of the State of Franklin. The sympathies of the people were aroused for one who had done so much to secure their independence by his heroism in bloody and successful battles with British, Tories and Indians. The court house was crowded with his friends, McDowells, and others, who had been with him at the defeat of Ferguson; a fleet horse had been prepared for him a short distance from the court house, of which he was informed, a signal given, and he quietly and uninterrupted walked out of the room, made his escape, and the matter dropped.

Among the first settlers of Burke county of whom I had either personal knowledge or from information received from old residents during my early years, were the McDowells, Bowmans, Greenlees, Erwins, Averys, Pickens, Carsons, Morrisons, Tates, Hemphills, Murphys, Perkins, Hildebrands, Caldwells, Pearsons, Forneys, Walkers, Brittains, Newlands, Collins, Millers, Lenoirs, McEntires, Waltons, Stevelies, Duckworths, Ballews, Bouchelles, and others too numerous to mention by name. These were men of mark, many of whom were distinguishd for their patriotism during the Revolution; others had won the esteem and respect of the people, as evidenced by their selection as representatives in congress, legislature, and offices of trust and profit of the county. Morganton, the county seat, was located shortly after the erection of the county in 1777, being nearly central, measuring from the crest of the Blue Ridge, and in some measure owing to the existence at that time of a small hamlet, settled before the Revolution, near the present residence of Mrs. C. M. Avery. Charles McDowell, senior, and Alexander Erwin were appointed Commissioners by the Legislature held at Newbern, 1777, to select a site, purchase or have donated land, to erect public buildings, etc., and a survey was made, a plot drawn, public square laid off, streets named, lots sold, and Morganton became a living town nine months after the Declaration of Independence. Professor Mitchel lof the University (who discovered that the Black Mountain was the highest east of the Rocky Mountains in the United States) in a published statement said Morganton was the most beautifully located town in the State.

The old court house was a frame building, used until the present building was completed, in 1835 or 1836, by James Binnie, a Scotchman, at a cost of $15,000. Owing to the distance from which the largest and best stone was hauled, from a quarry five miles distant, crossing Fleming's ford of the Catawba, with a team made up of a pair of oxen and a mule, making one load a day, caused a delay of several years before the building was completed, and, in consequence, the contractor was bankrupted. Col. I. T. Avery, R. C. Pearson, and Thomas Walton were Commissioners. A mason from Tennessee, who had a high reputation as a builder of fine edifices, made a proposition to build the court house of brick, on the plan of the stone one, for $10,000. I asked my father why Lyle's proposition was rejected, being cheaper, and, as I knew, he thought it would be handsomer. He replied in his usual facetious manner: "Pearson and I tried, but Col. Avery had stone in his head, and Pearson and I could not hammer it out."

The lawyers whom I saw and knew during my childhood, youth, and early manhood, and whose practice extended to many counties west of the Yadkin river were composed of many who had an exalted reputation for their skill and astuteness in conducting their cases, their legal attainments, brilliant oratory, and impressive arguments before a judge and jury. All now living, who knew the men, and resided within the bounds of their circuit, will not say that I have overdrawn the picture when I write the names of brothers Robert H. and Alfred Burton, Julius and Wallace Alexander, Joseph Wilson, David F. Caldwell, Bartlett Shipp, David L. Swain, Thomas Dews, Samuel Hillman, Jos. McD. Carson, Michael Hoke, B. S. Gaither, and others of later time, of the Morganton bar, who, if placed in the same constellation with those named, would only have added to its brilliancy. These distinguished men were in the court house at the time when the epitaphs were extemporized which have become historical. James R. Dodge was a near [nephew] relative of Washington Irving, the author of the "Sketch-book" in which he gives an account of the long sleep and its consequences of Rip Van-Winkle, a sobriquet that attaches to the "good old North State", however unjustly. Hillman, Dews and Swain, putting their heads together, concocted the following:

> *"Here lies James Dodge*
> *Who always dodged good,*
> *And never dodged evil;*
> *But after dodging all he could,*
> *He could not dodge the devil."*

Passing the paper to Dodge, he with repartee replied:

> *"Here lies Hillman and Swain;*
> *Their lot no man choose—*
> *For they lived in sin and died in pain,*
> *And the Devil got his Dews."*

The McDowells, Bowmans, and Greenlees came from Virginia to Burke country previous to the Revolution. [Late 1750] [Joseph McDowell's grant on Quaker Meadows was 1749]. They were all related by marriage or consanguinity. Joseph McDowell, senior was of Scotch descent, and emigrated from North Ireland to America. He was born in 1715 and emigrated with his wife at an early age, having offended his wife's relatives, the proud O'Neals, the descendants of the ancient Irish kings, by his marriage with their sister, Margaret O'Neal. Wheeler, in his History of North Carolina, writes as if they (Joseph and his wife) had only two sons, Generals Charles and Joseph. On the contrary there were four: Hugh, Charles, Joseph, and John. Charles died the owner of Quaker Meadows; Joseph died the owner of the fine plantation⁵ on Johns River, where the widow of the late Dr. Jno. McDowell lives. Dr. McDowell was grandson of Major [Joseph] McDowell, of Pleasant Gardens, the son of Hunting John McDowell, the brother of Joseph McDowell, senior. Hugh McDowell was the father of Margaret, who married Capt. James Murphy, and the only child, [John Hugh] was the offspring of this marriage. He married Margaret [Stringer] Avery, a niece of Col. Waightstill Avery, senior.

John Bowman, the husband of Grace Greenlee, came from Virginia about the same time as the McDowells and others. He was killed at the battle of Ramseur's Mills; he had but one child, a daughter, [Mary] who married William Tate, senior, of Hickory Grove, the old homestead of John Bowman; his widow, nee Grace Greenlee, married Gen. C. [Charles] McDowell. Major R. [Robert] McDowell Tate is the only living child of Wm. Tate, senior. James Greenlee, senior, owned the place on which I live, [Creekside] and was living there before and during the Revolution. He, by his thrift, foresight and industry, was possessed of large and valuable bodies of land in North Carolina and Tennessee. He had five sons by his wife, Mary Mitchell, who was his cousin, viz: Col. John M. Greenlee, Ephriam M., William, James, and David. He was regarded as the wealthiest man in the county. I remember an anecdote characteristic. On one occasion, during the war, a number of mounted Tories came to his house and demanded food for themselves and horses. It was in the fall; he pointed to a field containing about three acres, telling them to turn their horses in the corn; the Tories lived in the county and he knew them; noting their names, he quietly waited until the termination of the war. There was a move made to indict all Tories and confiscate their property. Mr. Greenlee made these men a domiciliary visit, calling to each one's recollection the raid made upon his premises; frightened, they readily came to terms, and doubtless the damages were fully satisfied.

John McDowell, fourth son of Joseph McDowell, senior, [Quaker Meadows] left two daughters; they married brothers, John and Robert McElrath, both of whom were good and highly respected citizens of this county. The extensive lands on which they lived and died, were inherited by their wives from their father.

The elder Greenlees, McDowells, Tates and many of their relatives and descendants, at their decease, were interred on an eminence overlooking the beautiful low grounds of Quaker Meadows and the adjacent lands of the Catawba. Col. Joseph McDowell, [Ash Hill] as well as his brother, Gen Charles, [of Quaker Meadows] were highly distinguished in the Revolution. They were very popular and held in high esteem by all who knew them. They were leading men in the days that tried men's courage and patriotism.

I have heard my mother speak in terms of the highest laudation of Gen. Joseph McDowell, his benevolence and sympathy with all suffering from any adversity; as a proof of this, he even shielded the Tories when the Whigs who had fought under his command (after the war) would threaten to maltreat and drive them out of the town. He would in words which they dared not disobey, command them to cease their persecutions; that the war was over, and we must live in peace and harmony. He died in 1801 at the early age of 45, and is buried by the side of his elder brother, General Charles McDowell. I went with his nephew, the late Capt. Charles McDowell, several years previous to the late war, to find his grave, thinking it might throw some light on a private matter in which we were personally interested. On a rough, unhewn stone, rudely carved, was his name. In a short time, if not already, the name will be obliterated, and the humble resting place of this hero and good man, can no longer be recognized. It will meet with the approbation of every good citizen of Burke county, if some members of this senatorial district, elected to the next Legislature, will ask the assembly to vote an appropriation for the erection of a monument to the memory of one who aided so much in obtaining the liberties we enjoy.

The life and character of Col. Waightstill Avery, his patriotism, love of liberty, and activity in all measures that availed to the beginning and success of the struggle for independence, have been so well set forth and portrayed in Wheeler's History of North Carolina, that I will only write of such incidents characteristic of his sterling worth, kindness of heart, benevolence, etc. His family, of English origin, emigrated early to the colonies and settled in New England, and are known there as the Averys of Groton. They must have been of Puritan stock, as the name Waightstill indicates. From a letter in the possession of a descendant of one of Col. Avery's brothers, dated "Groton, the 5th of ye 3 Mo. A.D. 1794", I learn that there were five — Lemuel, James, Latham, Isaac, and Waightstill. The writer, Latham, was a Quaker, his letter written in a beautiful, round hand and quaint style peculiar to his sect. In closing the long letter, he writes: "My son and daughter, with myself concluded last fall to set out to the Genesee country, and from that down to see Waightstill and thee; three times were set, but Providence forbid; so we laid it by. Desire to hear from thee. Inform us about Waightstill if thee can, of whom we have not heard these many years; Isaac, I remember thee. Latham Avery."

Waightstill and Isaac [Rev. Isaac never came to N. C.] are the ancestors of the North Carolina Averys, the remaining brothers of the New England States, and known, as before said, as the Averys of Groton. Two of the descendants of this branch of the family visited rela-

tives in North Carolina a short time previous to the late war; they
were ladies highly accomplished, Harriet and Lily Pumpelly.   The
former, after her return to New York, married Theodore Frelinghuy-
sen, who was a candidate for the Vice Presidency in 1844 on the Henry
Clay ticket. Isaac Avery, of Virginia, lived on the peninsula that divides York and James rivers, in Warwick county. He was an Episcopal
clergyman, and was ordained priest and deacon by Richard Yerrick,
Bishop of London, England, [Oct. 18] in 1769. His letters of ordina-
tion are now in the possession of his granddaughter, Harriet L. Walton, given to her by her mother, Margaret [Stringer] Murphy, nee
Avery. He preached before the revolution in the old Bethel church,
where the first battle of the late war was fought by the First Regiment
of North Carolina, under the command of Col. D. H. Hill. Isaac Avery
died in Norfolk, Va., and is buried in the Cross church, built in co-
lonial times. Col. Isaac T. Avery, [nephew] of Swan Ponds, was named for him.

Col. Waightstill Avery, after the death of his brother, invited his
orphan children to make their home with him. Embracing this affec-
tionate offer of their uncle, the two daughters, Margaret and Eliza,
lived happily until the marriage of Margaret to John Murphy; [1st
2nd John Collett]. Eliza afterward married Col. J. McK. O'Neal.

James Avery, the son of Isaac, came to North Carolina from Virginia with his sisters. He married a Miss [Elizabeth] Brown, of the
North Cove; she was a lovely character, esteemed by all who knew her.

Col. Waightstill was somewhat eccentric although full of the milk
of human kindness. He was in the habit of taking his dinner, when in
town, at my grandfather's, and was fond of a very rich pudding: before eating he would invariably ask the writer, "Does this pudding
have any butter in it? I cannot eat anything that has butter in it." The
servant, who was prompted, would answer, "Oh! no, sir." Eating heartily of the pudding, although rich in butter, he never discovered the
fact. My grandfather McEntire became blind several years before his
death, so that he couldn't read. His good friend, Col. Avery, sympathizing deeply with him on account of his bereavement, would read to
him for hours the newspapers of the time, always beginning with the
name of paper, where published, editor, date, etc., including every
item, and ending with the advertisements.

This benevolent kindness was highly appreciated and often spoken
of, and never forgotten by his family. Col. Avery was very fond of
honey and ate it in unusual quantities. On one occasion he met a
woman on the road as he was traveling; discovering she had a bucket
of honey he asked what she would charge for as much as he could eat.
Supposing he could not eat more than a pound, she said "Twelve and
a half cents." Getting off his horse, seating himself under a tree, he began eating from the bucket. The owner, seeing her honey was rapidly
diminishing, said: "Stranger, if you will stop, I will charge you noth-

ing for what you have eaten." "That was not the bargain," he said, finishing; he gave her double the amount promised.

It is well known that he and Andrew Jackson fought a duel, but the cause is not so well known. Col. Avery, in his practice of law, frequently referred to Lord Bacon's "Institutes" in proof of points made in his arguments in cases in the Superior courts in which he was employed, and always carried with him a large volume of this digest of English laws. Law books at the time were not so numerous as at this day.

Jackson and he were employed on opposite sides in the Superior court for Washington county. Expecting Col. Avery would refer in the course of the trial to this book, he quietly purloined it from the saddle bags, and after taking off the wrappings in which the book was infolded, substituted in its stead a flitch of bacon of the same size. Col. Avery, in the course of his argument, referred to the English law sustaining the point he had made. Removing the wrappings of the package he displayed to the astonishment and amusement of the august court and the attendants, a piece of real bacon. Suspecting Jackson as being the instigator of this practical joke, he denounced him as a poltroon and coward. These epithets, coming from a gentleman of the exalted standing and character of Col. Avery, stung Jackson to the quick. Jackson challenged him. They met (on what was called the field of honor) and exchanged shots, upon which the seconds interfered and the matter was satisfactorily settled. The original challenge is still preserved by Col. Avery's descendants. [See "Avery's of Groton].

My father's brother, William Walton, Jr., was a merchant living in the city of Charleston previous to 1808, and engaged in the African slave trade. He owned the plantation on Johns river (now owned by Jno. Sudderth's heirs.) He would send the negroes upon their arrival at the port of Charleston, to this place.

Col. Isaac T. Avery, the only son of Col. Waightstill, told me a remarkable incident of a slave, sent with others to this place, who had been brought from Africa: he would not associate with other negroes, but sought the company of intelligent whites. His father, Col. Waightstill, became interested in this man and asked him to come to see him at his residence — Swan Ponds. He did so, and said that he was educated; that he was of a nobler race than the Guinea negro, and was a leader among his tribe; that he was captured in a battle with another tribe and sold into slavery. Being asked if he could write, he said yes; he was given writing materials and wrote rapidly a sentence in Arabic; being translated, it proved to be from the Koran. He was dissatisfied and depressed in mind; finally writing to his master if he would let him return to Africa he would send him four men in his stead. He went to Charleston, his proposition was accepted, with directions to the captain of the vessel that the man was not to go ashore unattended until the terms were complied with. On the return to Charleston the captain was asked if he had brought the four men pledged. No, he had not; but explaining, said: "Before reaching Africa the man had so favorably impressed him that he would have let him go ashore with all the treasure in the possession of himself, on his promise to return; accordingly he went; in a short time he returned with $400 in gold dust (that being the amount necessary to buy four men), saying that he did not believe it right to send others into slavery that he might become free.

In connection with this perhaps exceptional instance of the uprightness, rectitude and fidelity of the negro, I cannot refrain from recording an instance, in part, of my own knowledge. In 1851, Robert McElrath, senior, for the purpose of paying his debts, which amounted to a considerable sum, sent by his son-in-law, G. P. Dodson, four negro men to the California gold fields. The negroes were to be more particularly under the guidance and direction of one of their number, "Uncle Jim", as he was called, who was skilled in placer mining, his master having confidence in his honesty and fidelity; they were to have one day in each week to mine for themselves. They were successful and made a considerable quantity of the precious metal. After diligently working for several years they returned by the way of New York. While in New York they were importuned by abolitionists to remain, gain their freedom and enjoy the fruits of their labor in California. Spurning this advice of dishonest white men, Uncle Jim returned with his treasure and the men under his care, to their rejoicing master "with their sheafs", greeted with the welcome plaudit, "Well done, good and faithful servants, enter thou into the joy of thy master and household." There were but few slaves that went with others, or their owners, that returned to slavery.

"Swan Ponds", the home of Col. Waightstill and his son (the only one) Col. Isaac T. Avery, was always distinguished for its profuse hospitality, and par excellence for the delightful entertainments enjoyed by young and old; and this may be truthfully said, to a large extent, of the homes of many citizens of "Auld Lang Syne". I can remember when a citizen might travel through the length and breadth of the county and could not offer to pay for a meal or night's lodging without insulting his host, unless it was a public boarding house.

Col. W. W. [Wm. Willoughby] Erwin, of "Belvedere", one of the most highly respected and useful citizens of the county, was a man of great dignity of person and manner; so much so, that young men when first meeting him became shy and diffident, which was speedily removed by his general affability. He was long clerk of the Superior Court, and was afterwards cashier of the first branch bank of the State established in Morganton, and no doubt the well known business talent of some of his living descendants and others, was inherited from him.

Col. James Erwin, of "Erwin's Delight," a cousin of the above Wm. W. Erwin, was also a highly esteemed citizen; he was for many years an efficient clerk of the county. He accumulated a handsome fortune. In some things he was peculiar. He was appointed guardian of James Murphy's grandchildren, who had inherited from their grand-father what was considered a large fortune in this part of the State at the time. After my marriage, in 1837, to the eldest of the heirs, he insisted upon resigning, and that I should take his place. Riding home with him shortly afterward, he said: "Tommy, my son, one of my neighbors said to Capt. Murphy (during his life) he believed little Jimmy Erwin was a little cracked. 'Well', said Murphy, 'if he is crack-ed, I never knew him to leak any.' But, my son, I leaked a little when I bought the Cherokee land." Impelled by this anecdote we both laughed heartily.

GENERAL ISRAEL PICKENS

Hon. Israel Pickens represented the county of Burke in the State Senate, 1808-9, and afterwards in Congress, 1811 to 1817. He was very popular and very much beloved by the people. He lived on the emin-ence known as "Vine Hill" (near where the splendid structure is being finished by the munificence of the State, for the education of the deaf and dumb), over looking the flourishing town of Morganton and the valley of the Catawba river, and a panoramic scene of "Where moun-tains rise and umbrageous dales descend", unsurpassed for magnifi-cence and beauty. On this attractive spot Mr. Pickens erected a pictur-esque building, in a measure comporting with its surroundings. After-wards, in turn, it was the residence of Col. John M. Greenlee and Col. B. S. Gaither. My father became the owner in 1842, and soon there-after pulled down the picturesque old house, cut down the grove of ancient oaks and the hedge of English hawthorn planted by Mr. Pick-ens. Expostulating with him, he said, "I did it for fear some one of my children might be so foolish as to live where wood and water could not be had without descending and ascending a mountain." Mr. Pickens removed to Alabama in 1817, and was subsequently [1st] governor of that state.

HON. FELIX WALKER

Hon. Felix Walker succeeded Pickens as member of Congress from this district from 1817 until 1823. Whilst canvassing the county on one occasion, addressing a large assemblage of people at the court house, he was charged by his competitor with being a Tory during the Revo-lution. Appealing to Capt. James Murphy, he asked whether they had fought as Whigs together. Murphy replied he did not so well remember the fighting but he did distinctly recollect their running together! This reply met with loud applause and Walker was elected.

HON. SAMUEL P. CARSON

Hon. Samuel P. Carson, son of Col. John Carson, of Pleasant Gar-dens, by his second wife, relict of Major Joseph McDowell, Jr., suc-ceeded Walker as a member of congress in 1825, and served continu-ously until 1833. Samuel P. Carson had only limited educational advantages, but he was a born orator; gifted with such forensic genius that the crowds of people whom he frequently addressed would be so enthused bv the glamor of his eloquence, as to become almost frantic with emotion and enthusiasm, impressed by his appeals to their patriotism, prejudices and passions. No man in Burke county, asking for political office, ever had more enthusiastic or faithful followers than Samuel P. Carson, until he endorsed and advocated, in a public speech, South Carolina's treasonable doctrine Nullification. In the winter of 1833, deserted by his old friends, he moved with his family to Arkansas.

THE CARSON-VANCE DUEL

His duel with Dr. R. B. Vance [Uncle of our Gov. Zebulon B. Vance] on the border of the Carolinas, at Saluda Gap, in 1827, resulted in the death of Vance in a short time, after receiving a mortal wound,—the only duel ever fought in Western North Carolina that terminated fatally. It was said at the time that Vance's last words were the following quotation from the tragedy of MacBeth:

> *"Out, out brief candle!*
> *Life's but a walking shadow; a poor player,*
> *That struts and frets his hour upon the stage,*
> *And then is heard no more; it is a tale*
> *Told by an idiot, full of sound and fury,*
> *Signifying nothing."*

Happily duelling, a relic of the feudal ages, has long been banished from the good old North State, frowned upon by her laws and all good citizens.

THE HEMPHILL FAMILY

The Hemphills of Silver Creek and Old Fort emigrated from the North of Ireland, previous to the Revolution. They were of Scotch descent, Presbyterians in religion, Whigs of the Revolution, and good, well-to-do citizens. I remember an anecdote told me in 1840 by a pensioned soldier of the olden time, in connection with the Silver Creek branch of the family. Ferguson, on his march from the Catawba to Gilbert Town, in 1780, had a chart of the country through which he was passing; on this chart was drawn an isolated mountain, directly on the line to Gilbert Town, to which he gave the name it now bears— "The Pilot Mountain". He was encamped near Mrs. Hemphill's; sending out a foraging party, they seized and carried to camp her flock of sheep. Mounting her horse she found Ferguson in his marquee.

He asked, "What can I do for you, madam?" She answered, "Col. Ferguson, I am told, and believe you to be a gentleman. Your men have taken all my sheep; winter is coming, and I have no means of clothing my little children except from the wool of my sheep." "Where is your husband?" "I will not tell you a lie, sir, he is out with the Whigs." "Well, madam, your husband is engaged in a rebellion against his lawful king, with others who are at war with me; but I am not

THE "WALTON HOUSE," BUILT BY JAMES McENTIRE (1748-1820)

HOME OF GOV. TODD R. CALDWELL, BUILT 1813

here to oppress women and children, but my soldiers must be fed; you may have half of the sheep." "May I take choice?" "Yes", said the colonel. With thanks, she left, following the orderly, who had been instructed, and, reaching the penned flock, she first selected the old bell wether, the leader of the flock for years, and, as was expected, the whole flock leaped the enclosure, following the flying leader home, and thus by her Irish forethought, outwitted the distinguished British colonel.

John Duckworth

John Duckworth was one of the few surviving soldiers of the Revolution in 1840. He was severely wounded in the battle of Ramseur's Mills, June 20, 1780. A large rifle ball which entered his left was cut from his right side in 1843, having carried this relic of the battle for sixty-three years. At a barbecue in Morganton in the Canvass for President in 1844, Gov. Morehead exhibited this bullet in the course of a speech made on that occasion, to a large assemblage of persons, producing a great sensation. Alexander Duckworth, his son, kept this relic as a precious heirloom. In illustration of the character of this old soldier and patriot, I have to refer to circumstances and incidents in which I took for the first time an active part in a presidential election. It was in 1840, before the county was divided into townships, when a large vote was always given in Morganton, I circulated a general notice that there would be a grand rally of the Whigs on the morning of the election at the forks of the Asheville and Rutherford roads, with refreshments of cakes and hard cider, and a large banner to be borne at the head of the procession by two Revolutionary soldiers, with this inscription painted in large letters upon the banner:

> *"In the sweat of our brows we earn our bread,*
> *And vote for Harrison, Tyler, and Morehead!"*

I consulted my father (Thomas Walton), who had been for many years agent for paying pensioners of the Revolution. He said there were only two living—John Duckworth, of Hunting Creek, and George Hodge, of Muddy Creek. Writing, I invited them to come to my house the evening previous to the election. Duckworth came first, and inquired who was to carry the banner with him. I replied, "George Hodge." "He was a Tory; I will carry no Whig banner with him," said Duckworth. I said, "Mr. Duckworth, you are certainly mistaken; he has been receiving a pension for many years." "Well, he ought not. I know he was a Tory." I said, "This will place me in a very unpleasant dilemma. Mr. Hodge will be here in a short time. He is a man of respectability and well off; he will be my guest. I have invited him, what am I to do?" "I don't know, but I won't carry the banner with him," Duckworth insisted. Seeing no other way to overcome the difficulty, I proposed that after supper I would suggest to them to tell me some incidents of the war, and that Duckworth could then charge Hodge with having been a Tory. "I'll do it," was the answer. When Mr.

RESORT HOTEL SEVEN MILES FROM MORGANTON BUILT BY
COL. WALTON IN 1878

HOME OF THOMAS WALTON (1782-1859), 2D POSTMASTER OF
MORGANTON IN 1803; AND THE SECOND OR THIRD SHERIFF
OF BURKE ABOUT 1790

Hodge came Duckworth treated him very coolly. After supper I asked them to tell me about the part they took in the old war, hoping that Hodge would satisfy Duckworth that he was on the right side. After some conversation Mr. Duckworth said, "Were you ever in Ferguson's camp?" "Yes, sir," said Hodge. "When and where?" said Duckworth. "After the battle of King's Mountain was over I went with other Whigs to see the dead Col. Ferguson; he was shot under the right eye," said Hodge. "That is true," said Duckworth, "but you were in Ferguson's camp at another time, when you took his foragers to Mrs. Hemphill's and took her sheep." "It is a lie, whoever says it." Duckworth sprung to his feet, and there would hvae been a collision between these game-cocks but for my interposition. Hodge said, "Duckworth, you know none but Whigs went when Gen. Griffith Rutherford called for volunteers to crush the Cherokee Indians, who were gathering their warriors to join the British and Tories. I have my discharge after the suppression of the Cherokees." Duckworth made no reply. Early next morning I asked Duckworth if Hodge had satisfied him. An emphatic "No" was the answer. I then went to Hodge and told him the banner was heavy and I thought it would be best to get a young man representing the Whigs of the day, to assist in bearing it, and as Duckworth was better known in this neighborhood, it would be better policy that he should represent the Whigs of the Revolution. "As for yourself," I said, "you shall have a prominent place in the procession. I am satisfied you were as good a patriot as Duckworth." He replied, "Oh, it makes no difference to me; I am now and have always been a Whig. I will take any place in the procession you may like."

AN OLD TIME ELECTION

Going early to the place designated, I found a large crowd assembled, having had printed in large letters on a strip of white paper (to be used as hat bands) the words, "No Sub-Treasury — No Negro Testimony", two of the many charges made by his opponents against Van Buren. I called upon the crowd to put the bands around their hats. They refused, saying that would be making "collar men" of them. I said, "Here is an old soldier who put, with other Whigs, a strip of white paper around their hats at the battle of Ramseur's Mills, to distinguish them from the Tories," "That is so," said Duckworth, "I was a Whig then and now; give me one." This caused a general rush for the strips and their hats were decorated with this denunciation of the Democratic candidates.

RANSOM HERNE

About this time a very laughable occurrence took place. Ransom Herne (whom many will remember) had for years indulged too freely in the "overjoyful" but had been converted, under the thrilling eloquence of a distinguished temperance lecturer, signed a pledge of total abstinence, and had determined to abandon the old habit. On a table near him was a keg of whiskey with the bung open. Jostled by the crowd the keg turned, and its contents began rapidly running out. As quick as a thought Ransom sprung and righted the keg.

"Why, Ransom", I exclaimed, "You, a strict temperance man to be guilty of saving pernicious poison." With downcast look, he said, "Squire, I knew it was wrong, but I could not help hating to see it wasted." Loud laughter and jeering ensued at his expense. A long column, two deep, was then formed, the banner in front borne by Duckworth and George Nail, the procession shouting and singing the old log cabin and hard cider songs, without breaking ranks, entered the court room (where the election was then held up stairs) at the north and passed out at the south, having deposited their votes for the Whig candidates (while passing the judge's stand in procession) to the utter dismay of the Van Burenites.

ROBERT CALDWELL

Robert Caldwell, Sr., was engaged in the Irish rebellion of 1798, and in consequence was banished and came to the United States the same year. One of his sons, Robert, at the time was serving an apprenticeship in some trade or business; the term not having expired, the rest of the family did not come to America until 1801. Mr. Caldwell, Sr., had two sons, Robert and John, and four daughters, Elizabeth, the ancestress of the Silver Creek Pearsons, Jane, who married James C. Smythe, who died without issue. Mary, who married Alfred Perkins, and Sidney, who married Elisha P. Miller. Robert, Jr., at first a clerk, afterward a partner with a merchant in the city of Petersburg, Va., acquired a considerable fortune, having gained the confidence and esteem of his partner; he died a bachelor in the prime of life. John married Hannah Pickett Robinson, was a merchant of Morganton, a man of large fortune; acquired in the main by intelligence, thrift and honesty; securing by these traits of character the respect and esteem of the best people of the county. I doubt if a more honest man ever lived. As an illustration, before he was a merchant, and with small means, he went with his wagon loaded with produce, on a visit to his brother at Petersburg. Having disposed of his load, his brother said: "John, instead of returning home with an empty wagon, why don't you buy goods and try your hand as a merchant?" He replied, "How can I buy goods without money?" The response was, "We will sell to you on six months time." Reluctantly he agreed to do so, and said he would call for the goods next morning. Failing to come at the time appointed, Robert mounted his horse, went to his camp and found he had gone; pursuing several miles he overtook him and after much persuasion, he finally returned to Petersburg and took the goods. Six months having nearly expired, and not having sold enough to discharge his indebtedness, he rapidly sold the remainder of the goods at less than cost. The amount due for the purchase of the goods collected in Spanish milled dollars, was packed with beeswax in a barrel, and transported in his wagon to Petersburg, where he discharged his note on the day it fell due. Mr. Caldwell, like all the Irish I ever knew, was not lacking in temper, particularly when believing some injustice or injury was about to be done to his fellow man or himself. At such times he became excited and would use language somewhat profane. I remember an anecdote on this line told me by his nephew, R. C. Pearson, who at the time, was studying Latin and boarding with his uncle. One of the leading physicians had sent a medical bill, and among the items was one rendered in Latin (?): "Dens extractor pro Carolina $2.00. "Mr. Caldwell, after scanning the charge for sometime, called out: "Come here, Robert, you have been taught Latin—what does this mean?" "Pulling teeth for Carolina, uncle." "Damn his 'Dens extractor pro Carolina'—who told him to pull teeth for Carolina?" (Carolina was a negress.) Another amusing scene took place in which Mr. Caldwell was an actor. A circus had come to Morganton, one of the first ever seen in the country. A large pavillion was erected, and an immense crowd had gathered, composed of men, women and children, of all classes. After the performance had fairly begun, the ring-master brought in what seemed to be a very vicious horse. Mr. Caldwell and a school teacher and poet named "Gamaliel Zelotes Adams" (who was regarded as a "crankish dude") were standing together near the entrance. The ring-master said the horse had not been and could not be ridden; and a handsome reward would be given to any person present who could mount, and ride him. No one seemed inclined to win the reward, until a countryman wearing a suit of well worn blue jeans and slouched wool hat, came reeling into the circus, apparently very drunk, swearing he could and would ride the horse. The horse was very much excited, showing his teeth, and kicking as the man staggered toward him. The ringmaster telling him, "You drunken fool, the horse will kill you." The man persisting, the ring-master proclaimed he would not waste further time with the fool, and if there was any one present who felt any interest in the man they had best take him away. Mr. Caldwell said, "Adams, if you will help me, we will take him out. The fool will have his neck broken if he mounts that horse." Adams assenting, they entered the ring, and seized the man, a struggle ensued which lasted some time, until overcome and exhausted by their exertions they released him, Mr. Caldwell saying, "Let the damn fool go to hell." Seizing the horse by his long mane, after several efforts the fool succeeded in getting his leg over the back of the plunging charger. Messrs. Caldwell and Adams (to whom my attention was directed) looked on amazed to see the rider get on his knees and finally on his feet, and disrobing himself of his sham attire, appeared in all the gilt and dress of the best bare-back rider of the circus. There were but two persons in the vast crowd that did not join in the laughter and thunderous applause that followed this clever trick. To Mr. C. and Mr. A's credit be it said that they were not the only ones deceived by a large number, but were the only persons present, who moved by philanthropy and goodness of heart, interfered only for fear that serious injury or death might happen to a human being, although to them a stranger, evincing the same spirit that influenced "the good Samaritan."

Mrs. H. P. R. Caldwell, his wife, in many respects one of the noblest women I ever knew, of good family, of masculine mind, refined and benevolent, loved by her neighbors. No one needy ever left her hospitable mansion unrelieved; and yet with a quick temper, if she detected anything bordering on duplicity or penuriousness in another, she did not fail to give them a piece of her mind; in a way they would not forget. For instance, on one occasion a man sent to her mill, wheat that was not well cleaned, and had to be screened. Previous to this he had sent logs to be sawed. Upon getting his flour home, he sent back asking for the screenings; the screenings were sent with her compliments, saying he could also have his sawdust. She had great presence of mind, a rare gift not common to her sex. When I was a boy twelve years old, Mrs. Caldwell, who was a good rider, came to town on horseback with her son Tod on his pony. Being invited to go home with them, Tod insisted upon my riding the pony while he rode with his mother. When we reached Fleming's Ford on the Catawba, river, she stopped and asked me if I had ever ridden across the river by myself. I said no, but I was not afraid. Directing me to keep above her, I went boldly in. The water ran swiftly, and the pony soon seemed to me to be going up stream. I pulled hard as I could turning in the opposite direction and seeing that I would soon be off the course, Mrs. Caldwell straightened me in the saddle, and said in an angry tone, "If you don't shut your eyes, Tom, and keep them shut until we get across the river, I will whip you severely." Badly frightened, I closed them instantly, believing she would certainly punish me if I disobeyed her, and we soon crossed the river safely. Mrs. Caldwell at this time was the owner of the valuable plantation on Upper Creek named "Cherryfields", on account of the large growth and quantity, of this species of timber, on the lowlands, a sure indication of the depth and fertility of the soil. There were born to these good people three sons and three daughters, Robert, Tod R., and James; Martha, Jane [2nd wife of John Collett], and Cornelia, only the youngest, Mrs. Lawson Henderson, surviving and living at the old homestead. The surname of this old family has become extinct in this county. Robert dying at an early age, James, a bachelor, a few years after his brother. Governor Tod R. Caldwell (hoping to perpetuate the family name) called his only son John. This promising and gallant lad was killed in battle on the march to Gettysburg, a blow from which his father never recovered.

THE PERKINS FAMILY

The Perkins family, of Johns river, descended from a native of England, who came to the Colonies in 1732. Landing in Pennsylvania, he removed to Lincoln county, North Carolina (then Tryon), founded in 1779. By way of pre-eminence, he was known as "Gentleman John Perkins." Accompanying an exploring party, led by a Moravian Bishop (from Salem, now in Stokes county, the "United Brethren" having built a church there in 1763), before any grants had been issued for the rich alluvial lands of Johns river and Lower creek, which were then still untilled and unoccupied. Availing himself of this fact, he obtained grants from the State for large bodies of the best land in Western North Carolina, devising the same to his six (a) sons, Ephriam, Joseph, John, Alexander, Eli and Elisha, and a daughter, Mary, whose offspring still own and live on them. The broad lowlands, having been cultivated in the various cereals for more than a century, without the use of fertilizers, show but little, if any loss from the original productiveness. The name John's River was derived from "Gentleman John", perpetuating his name as long as flows the limpid water of this beautiful stream, from its source near the eastern base of the Grandfather Mountain, (said by distinguished geologists to be the oldest, visible, earthly formation as yet discovered.) Joseph Perkins married Melissa Lavender, a niece of Mrs. Avery and protege of Col. Waightstill Avery, Sr. She was of French descent, probably Huguenot. (The name La'Vender has possibly been anglised from La'Vendee, a maritime department in the west of France) by whom Joseph had three sons, Dr. James Hervey, Osborne, and William, and five daughters, Elizabeth, who married Allen Connelly, Myra, who married Allen's brother, George Connelly, Mary was wife of David Corpening, Leah married Wm. Locke Baird and Selena, wife of Levi Laxton, James Hervey and William died unmarried. John Perkins, Jr. married Nancy Abernethy, who was a niece of the wife of General Peter Forney of Lincoln county, a soldier of the Revolution. The maiden name of his wife was Nancy Abernethy, Mrs. Perkins being probably her name-sake. Mr. Perkins died, leaving but one child, Susan, heiress to a large fortune in land and slaves. She married R. V. Michaux, a lawyer, who came to Burke in 1834 from Virginia. He was a relative of the distinguished North Carolinian, Nathaniel Macon.

Alexander Perkins married a Miss Rebecca Moore (a connection of Dr. Bouchelle). By her he had three children, two sons, Theodore and Thaddeus, and daughter, Clarissa. The only surviving member of this branch of the Perkins family is Thaddeus, Jr., and his family, who are the sole owners of the splendid domain on Wilson's Creek and John's river. Alexander and his brother John were the first to introduce horses of good pedigree and blood in Burke county, breeding from celebrated stock in Virginia, belonging to William Amis and Col. Johnson. They took great pains in training them, and delighted in showing their superiority in fleetness and bottom at long distances on the Quaker Meadows and other race courses, over the scrubs of the country.

Elisha Perkins, the eldest son of "Gentleman John" (the father of Alfred Perkins) inherited from his father the fine alluvial lowlands on the west side of John's river, about three miles from its mouth.

(a) The Perkins family history gives the following ten children: Elisha 1760, Mary 1762, Ephrain 1764; John 1767; Joseph 1768; Alexander 1774; Eli 1766; Burwell 1771; Sarah 1776; and Ann 1780.

He died at an early age, leaving a widow and two sons, Alfred and John, also 3 daughters. The widow married Major Highland who had distinguished himself during the war of the Revolution, in battles fought against the British and Tories, and was wounded at the battle of Ramseur's Mill.

Alfred Perkins, a man highly esteemed for his probity, was a leading elder in the Presbyterian church. His death in the meridian of life, was deeply regretted by all who knew him. He, like all the older members of the Perkins family, was of the bone and sinew of the land. He married Mary, the youngest [?] daughter of Robert Caldwell, Sr., leaving at his death, three children, Elisha Alexander, Robert C. and Jane Elizabeth. Alexander reminds me very much of his father in character, form and face.

> *"So near approach we their celestial kind*
> *By justice, truth, add probity of mind."*

Parson Miller

Mary, the daughter of John Perkins, Sr., married the Rev. Robert Johnson Miller, a native of Scotland, a clergyman of the Episcopal church, a high-toned gentleman of the old school, dignified and blunt in manner like most Scotsmen I have known, yet benevolent and kind.

He joined in marriage the descendants of the old pioneers, and Baptised their children, and prayed that God's blessing might rest upon them. He married my father and mother in 1803. His dress at that time was knee breeches, black silk stockings, low shoes, with silver knee and shoe buckles. He had a rubicund complexion and powdered hair. Thus he stood, prayer book in hand, a fine specimen of an English parson, of Goldsmith's days:

> *"A man he was to all the country dear*
> *And passing rich with forty pounds a year."*

He lived on a plantation left to his wife, Mary Perkins on Lower creek, [Caldwell Co.] his residence near the road side named after his wife, "Mary's Grove." I remember his baptising a child of one of Burke's leading citizens, who prided himself in always redeeming his pledges. (In similar cases many I fear do not feel the responsibility resting upon them, in becoming sponsors for children and taking upon themselves the solemn vows and promises required in baptism). A large assemblage of persons were present, in what was then a part of the present building of the Presbyterian church. After the usual preliminary prayers, etc., preceding the promises to be made by the Godfather and mother, the question: "Dost thou, in the name of this child, renounce the devil and all his works, the vain pomp and glory of the world? and so on to the end. To the astonishment of the congregation the response came from the father, loud and distinct, "I do not, sir" The parson looked at him sorrowfully in the face and said, "you will on the part of your child?" He replied, "I will on his part." "I wish you could say as much for yourself," said the parson. This is the only instance on record, so far as I know, where the matter had proceeded, as far as in this case, where the parent could not conscientiously, and therefore would not, make a promise which he did not intend to fulfill—to his credit be it said.

Alexander Perkins, the brother-in-law of Parson Miller, was a profane man, and frequently sorely tried the patience of the good man. Illustrating this, on one occasion, he got the upper hand of the parson. He was on the way to market, with a heavily loaded wagon drawn by a team of spirited horses. The public road passed in front and near the parson's residence, near the summit of a hill. The horses, refusing to pull. Perkins, irritated, beating the horses, cursing and swearing, brought the parson out. And rebuking him for his profanity, he said: "Brother Alex, don't you see that all this abuse of the dumb brutes, and the taking the name of your Maker in vain, does no good? Why, then, do you persist in doing so?" "Well", he said, "parson, that is so. I have tried cursing and beating them with no effect. Now you get down on your knees and pray and let us see if that will make the horses pull the wagon up the hill." Leaving in disgust, he said, "Perkins, you are a depraved, incorrigible man." Mr. Miller left two [3] daughters, one of whom, Margaret, married John S. Sudderth. The sons were Elisha P., Wm. S., Robert J., Eli W., Jno. W., Geo. O. and Nelson. The oldest, Elisha, married Sydney, the youngest daughter of Robert Caldwell, Sr. He was very popular and was elected to the State Legislature from Burke in 1836-38, from Caldwell in 1844-48.

THE CORPENING FAMILY

Albert Corpening, a native of the Netherlands, settled in Pennsylvania and married a lady of German parentage, Barbara Propst. He removed to Burke county about the year 1777. Purchased a large tract of land on Johns river from the heirs of Gen. Joseph McDowell, [Really from Joseph, Ash Hill] on which Gen. McDowell lived at the time of his death in 1801. Mr. Corpening was the ancestor of five sons—John, George, Jacob, Abram, and David, all of whom were respectable, industrious, well-to-do farmers of ample means, owning good lands on the Catawba, Linville and John's rivers and Lower creek. All of the name of Corpening of this county are descendants of these five brothers. Mr. Albert Corpening had one daughter, Mary, who was the wife of Major Forney of Upper Creek. Mrs. Forney was known for all those good qualities, industry, thrift, hospitality and benevolence, characteristic of the better class of Germans.

DAVID CORPENING

David Corpening, the youngest of the Corpening family, married Mary, a daughter of Joseph Perkins, and inherited the Johns river plantation from his father, Albert; a warm friend of mine, a man of sterling worth, remarkable for his strong common sense, high moral character; and was in my opinion, and in that of many others, one of the best and most skillful farmers of the county. I was guardian of two of his daughters. He was happily married to a lady, who was a help-meet in the true sense of the word. I have attended many sales of the property of deceased persons in Burke county, but never one evincing so much order, care, thrift and prosperity as his. A house erected for the purpose, neatly kept and filled with cloth of home manufacture, flax, tow and cotton, baskets and other useful utensils of the farm, gamon sticks of white oak, drawn and shaped by his own hand, ready for use at hog killing time, every article, tool and implement used in the cultivation of the land, clean, bright, and in perfect order, a place for all and all in its proper place. Well, did he deserve the name of a model farmer.

THE BALLEW FAMILY

The Ballews of Burke, old pioneers and ancestors of numerous descendants now living in McDowell, Caldwell and Burke, were of French origin. The spelling of the name anglicised the original ortho graphy, which was Ballou. From this paternal and maternal ancestry have sprung the Ballews of Caldwell, the Rutherfords and Rusts of Burke and the Connellys of McDowell and Caldwell. They were all, so far as I know and have been informed, good religious, moral, highly respectable citizens of this county previous to the forming of Caldwell and McDowell, sustaining in all the walks of life those characteristics that make the good citizen. Peter Ballew, the ancestor of the Caldwell branch, was elected to the State Lgislature in the commons of 1825 and to the Senate in 1835.

JOHN RUTHERFORD
The Work Of Dr. Abernethy

John Rutherford, Sr., of Bridgewater, married Nancy [Susannah] Ballew, by whom he had five children, two sons and three daughters —John, Robert, Nancy, Celia and Jane. John Rutherford, Jr., one of the wealthiest of Burke's citizens, was in many respects a re markable man. He was somewhat quaint and eccentric. He was well read in history and light literature. His place he named after the Earl of Bridgewater (not, as many suppose, because he built a bridge cross-ing Muddy creek, leading to his residence.) With three maiden sisters he lived a bachelor until he was 80 years old or more. Noted for his hospitality and benevolence, he endowed the college named for him, founded by its successful president, R. L. Abernethy, who deserves credit, almost beyond words to express, for having given, and continu-ing to give, an education to young men and women, fitting them for any vocation in life (so far as depends upon education) at a price so low as places it almost within the reach of all, and withall, making large personal sacrifices. By his laudable philanthropic exertions in this cause he deserves an eulogy more enduring than this brief notice.

Mr. Rutherford was near-sighted. Mr. Rutherford was myopic, be-ing what is commonly called near-sighted; so much so that he could not distinguish by form or feature his most intimate acquaintances, and, when meeting them, would never call their names until they had spoken. From long practice, and from the well-known fact that if one of the organs of the body is defective, another is strengthened correspondingly, he had become very expert in recognizing them either by the tone of voice, or enunciation of those with whom he associated, and would soon afterwards speak to them by name. His manner was such as led them to believe that he thought he had deceived them as to his eyesight being defective, and this attempt to deceive was practiced on his own family. In proof of this one of his sisters was asked by my mother, "Miss C., why don't you induce your brother to wear spectacles? They would be so useful and relieve him from his nearsightedness." She replied, "Oh! Mrs. Walton, I would not do so on any account for fear of offending him. He does not know or suspect that we are aware of this defect." W. B. Rust, Esq., near neighbor and maternal uncle, who, himself was near-sighted, and wore glasses, in speaking of this idiosyncracy of his nephew told me that once being in the room where Mr. R. had been writing a letter at his desk, unfinished, he, Rutherford, left the room. He concluded that if Mr. R. would only put on his (Rust's) specks, being adapted to his eyes and seeing the great advantage they would be to him, he would forego his prejudice against the use of them. Taking off his glasses and laying them on the desk near the letter in such a way as to know whether they had been moved, he left the room, and after remaining out some time returned. the letter was finished, sealed and directed, the spectacles untouched, lying as he had placed them. This unparalleled singularity was the cause of narrow escapes "by flood and field", some of which I shall omit. Crossing his bridge, on one occasion, he made a misstep, plunging ten feet into the turbid creek, fortunately but little hurt. Struggling to reach the shore, his wig which was not worn on account of baldness, came off. He never wore another after the loss of this. At the marriage of the Hon. Burton Craig to Elizabeth, the oldest daughter of Col. James Erwin, there were a number of guests gathered from several counties. Mr. Rutherford was one of them. He was fond of the ladies, and, owing to his defective sight, when addressing them, usually brought his face very close to theirs. The wedding over, he took a seat near a belle from the valley of the Yadkin, extending his arms as though he purposed to embrace the fair one. Alarmed, she sprang to her feet, crossed the room to a vacant corner, he following close with his long arms extended. Lightly dodging under them she made her escape, leaving the persistent pursuer, still with extended arms moving until striking the wall of the house, he found the bird had escaped and he was left standing, not cheered by the laughter of the merry crowd who had witnessed his discomfiture. Notwithstanding his eccentrics, he was possessed of so many good traits that he was held in the highest estimation by the best people of the county.

JOHN RUTHERFORD'S SISTERS

His sisters, Misses Nancy, Jane and Celia, were pious, amiable,

"Creekside," built by Col. Walton circa 1836

modest ladies. Miss Celia, the youngest, having associated more with other refined ladies of her set, was not so peculiar or eccentric as her sisters, who wore old-fashioned, long hood-shaped bonnets, of dark green silk, without bows, possibly indicating that they did not want to catch beaux. However, this may be they were much attached to their bowless bonnets, which were certainly attached to them. In proof of this I will give an incident. At home or abroad they were never seen without them. About the year 1829 or 1830, these good ladies made mother a visit and concluded, at her solicitation, to spend the night. At the time there were several young girls of "sweet sixteen" boarding at my father's going to school. One of these was full of curiosity (not unusual with her sex) and mischief, Eliza G. Tate, of "Hickory Grove", got permission to sleep in the same room with the Misses Rutherford in which there were two beds, determined as she said, to see whether they slept in their bonnets.

An Amusing Anecdote. The next day she gave the following account of what she witnessed: "I went to bed before they came up stairs. The fire was burning low when they entered the room. They sat down near the fire with bonnets on whispering in low tones. I thought they never would go to bed. Finally, the fire went out, they undressed, put on their night robes, bonnets 'status quo' on their heads; when lo! they blew the candle out and all was dark. I said to myself, 'Never mind, old gals, I'll catch you in the morning.' I waked early, it was hardly light, and behold! there they sat in their night gowns with their everlasting bonnets on." Miss Nancy was twice engaged to be married. When her first engaged lover came prompt at the appointed time, a change had come "o'er the spirit of her dreams." She said to him, "I am not ready; the pockets of my wedding gown are still unmade." The quondam lover left disgusted, never to return. The second was not more fortunate than the first.

He wouldn't swim. Reaching Morganton on his way to reach the abode of his intended bride on the evening of the day appointed for his wedding, he found it impossible to do so without risking his life by swimming the swollen waters of Silver and Muddy creeks. The next morning he hastened to explain and apologize. He found her in no fit mood to be appeased by explanations, apologies and regrets but sent the crestfallen lover off with this parting thrust of the tongue: "If I am not worth the swimming of two small streams, I am not worth having." Unless I am very much mistaken, a majority, if not all, of the fair sex who honor the writer by reading these reminiscences of the olden time, will agree if either of these cold lovers' hearts, had been pierced with cupid's darts he would not have been so easily repulsed, but enamoured, on bended knees, would have poured forth with suffused eyes, appeals of touching eloquence and fervidness, portraying the endless misery of his future life, caused by the cruel rejection of his proffered love. Her heart softened by these devotional appeals and by persistent perseverance afterward, the prospect for future success would have brightened, and possibly the dearest wish of his heart would have been realized.

DR. THOMAS BOUCHELLE

Dr. Thomas Bouchelle, one of Burke's oldest citizens, was of French descent. His name has become extinct in this county. His first wife, Mary Moore, was the mother of his five children, Slater, Bayard, Ensor, Matthis, Eleanor, and Elvira. Dr. Bouchelle evinced his French parentage by his joviality, affability, politeness and urbanity. He did the "honors of his house" with all the urbanity of his forefathers, was one of the most successful physicians this county ever had, rarely using, if ever, medicines concocted from mineral or poisonous substances, such as calomel, blue pill, strychnine and opium, the last named, in a diluted form. He was my father's, as well as my own family physician. I attribute his wonderful success in curing the sick more to his cheerful manner, and persuading his patients to believe that they were not seriously sick. Instead of putting on a long face, holding watch in hand, counting the pulsations of the heart and whispering that the patient was a very sick man, Bouchelle would approach the sick (who with flushed face and anxious look, was watching the doctor's countenance to see if there was any gleam of hope), saying, "Oh! my dear fellow, there is nothing serious the matter with you, your old uncle will soon have you out of bed," at the same time telling some humorous anecdotes in his inimitable way, would soon have the attendant household as well as the sick cheered and laughing. Physicians all agree from experiments made, that a man may die, or rather death may be produced from the force of imagination alone. Dr. Bouchelle died suddenly (as I once heard that Col. I. T. Avery said to a friend: "I want to die with my harness on.") while visiting a patient, universally regretted by all who knew him. He owned a beautiful bay horse, well cared for like her master. Full of life, no one was permitted to mount her, save the Doctor. Fanny had a habit of tossing her head up when touched with a whip. A day or two before his last marriage, in the exuberance of his spirit, he struck Fanny with his whip; snorting and throwing up her head, she knocked out his last remaining front tooth. Laughing, he said, he much regretted the loss, for the reason that he could no longer tell his wife he was not so old as to be without a single tooth. Mr. Gamewell, a distinguished Methodist preacher, paying the Doctor a visit, knocked at his door. The Doctor answering, Mr. Gamewell clasped his hand, saying, "Dr. Bouchelle, my name is Gamewell; my horse's name is Eatwell and he wants to be fed well." The Doctor responded, "Parson Gamewell, I hope you comewell, you and Eatwell shall be fedwell, welcome to the domicile of Dr. Thomas Bouchelle." Dr. Bouchelle had a large baldhead. He was asked if he did not suffer from the flies. "Why, no", he said, "my head is a first rate fly trap, if one lights upon it, his heels are tripped up and his neck is broken." There are other anecdotes of the bright old man too numerous for this publication.

MAJOR JACOB FORNEY

Major Jacob Forney, an old pioneer, was the son of Jacob Forney, who came to the United States from the Canton of Berne in Switzerland. Landing in Pennsylvania, he moved to Lincoln County, then Tryon, in 1754. He married a Swiss girl, Maria Bergner. By her he had three sons, Jacob, Peter, and Abram. Jacob, the eldest, was the owner of the splendid tract of land on Upper Creek, now divided and owned by his descendants. Major Jacob Forney, Jr., was one of the first settlers of Burke, and married Mary, the eldest daughter of Albert Corpening. His good wife, as well as himself, were much esteemed by the best people of the county. They lived happily together for many years, blest with a numerous family, enjoying life, and reaping the fruits of their probity and industry from their land, literally "flowing with milk and honey". At the time of his becoming a resident of Burke County game of every species abounded. The buffalo, elk, deer and the beaver had not been extinguished by the white man; and the Major would tell of his escape from a wounded buffalo by climbing a tree, rifle in hand, to a fork in the tree, and from this place of refuge shooting the mad bull. I have seen well defined traces of beaver dams at Col. Avery's place on North Toe river, and have been told by him that within his recollection, the last beaver caught in Burke county, was near this place, and the last elk was killed by Jonas Davenport, on a ridge leading to the Roan or Yellow mountain, named from that fact the Elk Hollow Ridge. Its horns were so ponderous that they were never removed, and were seen for many years afterwards. Major Forney, by his wife, Mary, had seven sons and four daughters, Thomas, Newton, Hervey Albert, Marquis de Lafayette, Bergner, Daniel, Fatimt, Mary, Sonora, and one other who died in childhood. Although marrying late in life he lived to see his children grown.

DANIEL FORNEY

Daniel, the youngest son, was the "bravest of the brave" I ever knew; giving evidence of this truth on more than one occasion during the late war. When the notorious Kirk captured Camp Vance in 1863, I was organizing a force of citizens to repel, as fast as could be done, his sacking the town. This he learned by some means. Hurriedly leaving the camp with his prisoners and plunder, he crossed the river and made a bee line for Tennessee by the way of the Sudderth place. Sending a mounted party of twenty five or thirty men and placing them under the command of Lieutenants Frank Craig and Thomas McEntire, who were here on a furlough from the army, I directed them to be governed by Daniel Forney in endeavoring to get ahead of Kirk, and by ambuscade annoy and hold him in check until the footmen could overtake him. Forney being familiar with the paths and near-cuts through the mountains, as well as the best points for attacking the enemy, succeeded in heading him at a gap on the south end of the Brown Mountain. Forney advised taking a position in a large cluster of alders, within 20 yards of the road, but the men (I believe) without dissent, said there was great danger of their force (small as compared with Kirk's) being captured. Kirk's forces were estimated at two thousand. Forney being overruled, the men took a position safer for them and nearer their horses. Kirk marching at the head of the column. When fired upon, his men, panic stricken, left the road. Kirk was shot in the arm, and a number of the prisoners escaped. I was afterwards shown by Mr. Forney where he had proposed to place his men. It looked to me hazardous, but he would have run the risk and, being so near, Kirk would in all probability have been killed. About the time of General Lee's surrender four raiders, said to belong to Vaughn's Tennessee command, were passing through the country taking the best horses and mules from the people by force of arms. Having robbed Mr. Hunt, who lived at Quaker Meadows at the time, they learned from some bad persons that Daniel Forney had a fine mare. It was dark when they reached his house which was enclosed by a plank fence. A large gate led to the stable. They rode up to the fence and halloed. Forney, coming out, asked what they wanted.

"We want your mare."

"You'll not get her," responded Forney. "If you attempt to go through that gate some of you will be shot."

Immediately they commenced firing at him with their revolvers. Forney never flinched, but returned the fire with his double-barrel shot-gun charged with buckshot. At length one of the marauders called out, "Oh, Lord! I am killed; don't shoot any more." Sending for his neighbor, Dr. [John C.] McDowell, they went in pursuit and found the rascals at Cherry Fields in an out house of Mrs. Caldwell's. The wounded man, unable to ride, compelled them to stop. They were armed with Colt's army revolvers, and had a considerable amount of greenbacks, the first I had ever seen. The wounded man had received eight or ten buckshot in the face and breast. I told Daniel his gun was not good or the man would have been killed. He said he could only account for it by its having been loaded for a long time and the powder had lost its strength. I don't hesitate to say that there is not one man in ten, under all the circumstances, that would not have surrendered the mare. It is an old saying that "blood will tell whether in man or beast." In Forney's veins coursed the blood of his grandfather, Jacob Forney, Sr., who according to Wheeler's history, at one time kept at bay twelve or fifteen Indians for several hours, protecting his wounded friends until a fort two miles distant was safely reached. Jacob Forney, Jr., was born 1754, died 1840. Mary, his wife, born 1788, died 1867. Both were buried at the old homestead.

BRICE COLLINS

Brice Collins was a popular man of the old school, and was elected a member of the State Legislature nine times. In 1805 and 1806, with

Col. John Carson; with David Tate in 1807, and almost consecutively from 1812-1822, the sessions being held annually, until made biennial by a change of the constitution in 1835. He owned and lived on a plantation on Johns River known as the Collins' place, about eight miles from Morganton, where his body, attended by numerous friends and neighbors, was buried in 1834, with Masonic honors. Mr. Collins was a brother-in-law of Dr. Bouchelle. His wife was a Miss Jemima Moore. She and the doctor's wife were sisters. By her he had two sons and two daughters, DeLafayette and James Monroe and Elinor and Elvira. The name Lafayette became very common in this county. The good people of "Auld Lang Syne", moved by sentiments of affection and gratitude for one who had contributed so much financially and by great risk of life in freeing the colonies from the British yoke, were desirous of perpetuating his name in their own families; not being aware that they were giving their children a nobleman's title, instead of his simple Christian and surname Gilbert Motier.

NAME NO MORE CHILDREN AFTER ME

Most men regard it as a compliment to have children named for them. I never heard of but one instance where a man (who was a distinguished judge) objected to it. As I remember, this occurred at a court held in the town of Greensboro. Judge Saunders was presiding. A man was arraigned, tried on an indictment for larceny. (This was previous to the abolition of the whipping post), and found guilty. His given name was Romolus Mitchell Saunders. The court room was crowded, and the judge, excited, said, "Hear all you people present; when you go home, tell your wives and neighbors to name no more children after me. Consider the situation in which I am placed; compelled, in discharge of my duty, to pass sentence on this poor wretch to receive thirty-nine lashes on his bare back, and he is a man bearing my full name, Romulus Mitchell Saunders."

A TERRIBLE EXPERIENCE

Mr. Collins was of striking physique, robust and muscular. On one occasion being with a large pleasure party on the Table Rock, Dr. Bouchelle was anxious to take a peep over the awe inspiring perpendicular precipice, 300 feet high and of solid rock. On the northeast end, prostrated, he crawled to the edge, Collins following, seized him by the feet and pushing him over as far as he could reach without losing his balance, called out, "Now you go, you old rascal, I always wanted Polly (Dr. Bouchelle's wife)." If any one wants to know exactly how the Doctor felt they will have to undergo the strain upon the nervous system. It is an unquestioned fact that extreme fright will make the hair of the head stand erect "like the quills on the fretful porcupine", and turn white in a few hours. Whether this was the cause of the Doctor's, not only turning white, but his extreme baldness, is a question unanswered. The immense size, form and altitude of the

Table Rock (5,000 feet above sea level), the magnificent picturesque and extensive view it commands from its summit, has caused the visitations of thousands in the past and doubtless will cause to come to it thousands in all time to come.

JOHN HENRY STEVELIE

John Henry Stevelie, a native of Switzerland, was born in 1747 and died 1836. His wife, Barbara, was born 1742 and died 1821. He emigrated to the United States shortly after the Revolution and settled in Morganton, Burke county. He ranked with the best citizens, and was a merchant for many years. About 1818, he moved to a plantation near town, purchased from Daniel Morgan, and built a brick house, which is still standing and is now the residence of George Phifer, Esq. Mr. Stevelie was well educated and wealthy. I remember being at his house when a child with my parents, during the life of Mrs. Stevelie. We were regaled on cake and sangaree. The cake was baked in a corrugated copper pan, in the form of a turban, brought from Switzerland by Mrs. Stevelie a hundred years ago. After her decease my mother became the owner. There never was a wedding of the elite in the land afterwards that this old relic was not used to give form to the bridal cake. It is still in use.

BEAUTIFUL DRESSES

Mrs. Stevelie's dresses, made in the old style and of brocaded silk, are in the possession of the Erwin family and still used by the ladies of Morganton in tableaux, etc. Mr. Stevelie proved the estimation in which he was regarded by the old people by being elected to the Senate of the Legislature in 1804, 1805, and 1806. The remains of himself and wife, marked by two rough hewn stones, rest side by side, on the top of "Morgan's Hill" unenclosed, and overgrown with briars and brushwood. Rudely carved on a gray stone are the following lines; no doubt composed and written by Mr. Stevelie, who survived his wife fifteen years:

> *"Go home, my friends, wipe off your tears,*
> *I must lie here until Christ appears.*
> *When He appears then I will rise*
> *And view you with immortal eyes."*

A WORTHY CAUSE

Will not the merchants of Morganton and others of the county contribute each a trifle to have the remains of these, who during life were so much esteemed and respected by the citizens of Burke, removed to the cemetery? There they will be cared for and undisturbed by the ploughshare.

FIRST INSURANCE LAW IN THIS STATE

By an act of the General Assembly of North Carolina, held at Raleigh, November, 1803, John Henry Stevelie and David Tate, Sr., were appointed to open books for receiving subscriptions to a Mutual Insurance Society against losses by fire, etc., (See Act, chap. IV, 1804) this being (I suppose) the first insurance act ever passed by the State.

PEDDLING

At the same session, 1803, merchants and peddlers were taxed somewhat differently than at present. Peddlers were required, under a penalty of twenty pounds, to obtain a license authorizing them to hawk or peddle goods, from any clerk of some county in the State, authorizing the peddler so to hawk and peddle in any and every county in the State. He was required to pay for the privilege the sum of ten pounds, to be accounted for by the clerk, to the use of the State. Merchants under this law were taxed, without regard to the amount invested, the sum of fifty shillings on each and every store, at which they shall sell goods, wares, etc.

The law, so favorable to the peddlers, gave a great impetus to that mode of trafficing, they having the right, under one license, to peddle in all counties in the State for 12 months. Many of them came from distant counties during the courts held in Burke, then covering so large a territory with but few stores. I have seen during court week, from the southwest corner of the public square on Union and Sterling streets to the intersection of Union and Greene streets, a crowd of their wagons, and others on the square, their goods displayed on temporary scaffolds, going off like hot cakes to a hungry crowd, many of them making a good living by their persistent energy and profits, and some of them fortunes.

JAMES PATTON, SR.

A well authenticated instance, I remember. James Patton, Sr., of Asheville, first settled in Wilkes county. Being comparatively poor, he began his pursuits of a fortune of hawking goods, from a knapsack, on foot, over the rough roads and rugged mountains of Western North Carolina, undeterred by the small returns he was day by day receiving. The gold coming slowly in; with eyes steadily fixed on the goal he was determined to reach it if fair dealing, indomitable will and perseverance could accomplish it. Crowned at length with success in his old age, he no doubt felt rewarded for all the toil and trouble he had undergone in contemplating the large fortune he had secured for his numerous family, among the most respectable of the county of Buncombe. Mr. Patton, like all Irish, had his share of caustic wit. On one occasion a neighbor, also from the Emerald Isle, who had come to the United States on the same vessel with Mr. Patton, was in his store at Asheville when Mr. Patton was receiving a large stock of goods. He said: "Jamie Patton, you have been a very lucky mon, sor; and you should be vary thankful to the good Being for his blessings. I can well remember when you were plodding on your feet with your trifle of goods on your back, and sure I was making ropes." The reply was characteristic: "Yes, yes, Mr. Bell, and you are making ropes still."

This peddling business was continued to a large extent for a quarter of a century. During the sessions of the Superior Court, Turner and Hughes, of Raleigh, would send by wagon books, historical, biographical, poetical, etc., and little Tom Scott, in his sulky, with trunk strapped on behind, filled with fine jewelry from Bemars and Dupuy's, of Raleigh. The beaux and ladies of the elite were always delighted at his arrival, the former having an opportunity of bestowing on their sweethearts a gaze or token of their love; its acceptance by the fair one an assurance of a blissful return.

Laughing Gas

In 1835, the old frame Court House was still standing. A traveling lecturer and chemist had advertised that a lecture would be given in the court room at night illustrated by interesting and amusing experiments such as producing water by a combination of "Hydrogen and Oxygen Gas", and other features instructive as well as amusing. He said he would close by administering to the audience "Laughing Gas", but none of the fair sex would be admitted. It being court week the room was crowded to its utmost capacity. The lecture was highly appreciated, as well as the chemical experiments and all were now anxious for the crowning enjoyment of the evening. Filling a large bladder with laughing gas, the chemist called for some one to come forward and partake of it, saying that it was perfectly harmless, that its inhalation would be delightful to the recipient, and its effect amusing to those who witnessed it. He said that the ruling passion at the time would be exhibited while the person was under its influence. After some hesitation a peddler by the name of Lewis presented himself. Under the instruction of the chemist he began inhaling very slowly. In less than a minute he seized the bladder with both hands and with dilated eyes and deep drawn breath, he lowered his body as the gas was exhaled. He clung to the bladder and it was wrenched from his grasp with difficulty. There was another peddler sitting in one of the lines of elevated seats used by lawyers in the center. Passing by all other persons, he caught his professional brother by the collar and commenced beating him in the face like a demon, until the effect of the gas passed off. A heavy, rather stupid-looking individual, with a large head and bull-like neck, was the next to imbibe, exhibiting all the delightful sensations as did Lewis, from inhaling the exhilarating compound. After the forcible taking away of the gas, he immediately walked to the rear of the room, like one in somnial slumber, striking his head, like a battering ram, with great force against the sealed wall, and continued to do so until taken away by some of the spectators who feared he would do himself some serious injury.

Ballew As A Butter

His head must have been sore next day, unless the skull was formed like that of a man I knew (and no doubt will be remembered by others now living) by the name of Ballew, of this county. He was famous as a butter with his head, and was known, for a wager, to have butted out the heads of four barrels. I never witnessed these feats; I "tell the tale as it was told to me." At one time he lost a bet made by one of his neighbors that he could beat a pet ram (famous for butting habits) at the ram's own game. The day was appointed, and the witnesses, with the principals, appeared on the field of battle. On one side of the lists there was a deep gully. In order to induce the ram to attack him, Ballew had to meet his opponent on all fours, so as to bring their heads in juxtaposition. Drawing lots for position Ballew's had to be taken near the gully. At the signal given they met in mid career, the ram knocking Ballew not only head overheels, but into the gully, and the ram was proclaimed the victor. Ballew's skull was remarkable. At the point where the skull joins the bones of the nose, to and above the natural opening of the skull at birth, his skull had a ridge of solid bone protruding perceptibly from the natural form of the skull, in some measure proving a shield in preventing concussion of the brain by a severe blow on the skull.

HON. PINCKNEY HENDERSON

Hon. Pinckney Henderson, who was the first governor of the "Lone Star State", was in Morganton soliciting aid in the war between Mexico and Texas. After inhaling the gas he mounted the rostum and delivered one of the most eloquent, fervid and impassioned harrangues ever delivered to a sympathizing people, lasting but a few minutes. He threw his hands to his head exclaiming, "Hello", looking confused and distrait, while the audience shouted with applause. There were many other scenes ridiculous and side-splitting, caused by the laughing gas that we, of necessity, are excluding from publication. Why call it "Laughing Gas"? Those who partake of it do not laugh; on the contrary it impels them or compels them to do in an earnest, serious way, only what the ruling passion at the time suggests, and the spectators alone are convulsed with laughter.

Reminiscences of the olden time of which I write are brought to mind principally after retiring for the night.

> *"Oft in the stilly night,*
> *Ere slumber's chain hath bound me;*
> *Fond memory brings the light,*
> *Of other days around me."*

GOLD FOUND

With winged speed, the news wafted abroad that gold had been discovered in Burke County. Brindle and wife brought the first product of their mine, about 80 pennyweights, to Morganton (which had been made in a short time by panning the earth and gravel without the aid of machinery.) This was the first gold ever made in Burke, and was sold to Thomas Walton, a merchant, at eighty cents per pennyweight. Brindle gave him a glowing account of the extent and richness of the mine. My father said, "If it is as you say, you have a large fortune in store for yourself and family; never sell your mine; you will find many shrewd men, who will persuade you to sell."

"No," said his wife, "He shall never sell it, not if they agree to cover the land with silver dollars." Paradoxical as it may seem, it not unfrequently happens that trifles light as gossamer succeed, when dollars fail, and such was the case of Mrs. Brindle. After long persistence in refusing to take five thousand dollars, offered by a company, which her husband had consented to take, provided she would assent, one of the company (knowing the fancy that the Dutch had for gaudy red colors), as a last resort took with him a brilliant old-fashioned red cassimere shawl, threw it around her shoulders, saying he would make her a present of the beautiful shawl, provided she would assent to the sale. The shawl was victorious. The mine was sold. Tens of thousands of dollars in gold was realized from Brindle's mine. The old piles of earth and gravel have been worked over three or four times.

Soon every creek, branch and tributary was prospected from John's river and Lower creek, including Second Broad river and its tributaries; taking the names in many instances of the original owners, such as Brindletown, Brackett Town, Jamestown, Huntsville and others more euphonious, such as Val Dor and Golden Valley, covering an area of more than thirty miles square. To this region flocked many like "eagles to the carcas", many from middle and eastern North Carolina. Men of note and wealth, buying the mines from their original owners — Burtons, Mangums, Hawkins, Greens, Robards, Alexanders, Willises, Norwoods, Weavers, Satterwhites, Thomases, Masseys, and many others, bringing their slaves with them; and some from Virginia, Hodges and Grahams, and others of Burke and Rutherford, were largely engaged in mining in this region for more than twenty years.

Immense quantities of the precious metal were taken from the mines during this time, and as there is no means of ever approximating the amount, it will never be known. I have known as much as thirty thousand dollars worth of gold taken from not as much as an acre of land at Jamestown by Col. Joseph Erwin, and W. F. McKesson, at comparatively a small amount expended for labor. Most of these miners had their families with them, lived extravagantly, thinking they had an inexhaustible fund in their mines; proving the old adage, "Come light; go light."

In proof of this belief, I remember an incident. Ex-Governor Hutchins Burton brought a large quantity of gold to the bank to be transmitted to the mint at Philadelphia, by the cashier, Col. Isaac T. Avery. Col. Avery congratulated him upon his being so successful in mining. He said, "Colonel, I want to take your advice whether I had not better curtail my mining operations for fear of reducing the price of gold; I verily believe I can make bushels of it." "Go ahead, Governor, make bushels of it if you can, I will guarantee you won't reduce the price one cent."

There being but one mint established by the government at the time, when so many were engaged in gold mining, the miners were at some trouble and expense in having their gold converted into a circulating medium.

CHRISTOPHER BECHTLER

A German named Christopher Bechtler had emigrated to the United States with his family, and settled about three miles from Rutherfordton, on the Jamestown road, about ten or twelve miles from the mines in 1833 or 1834. He proposed to the miners that he would flux, analyze and coin their gold for a small percentage. A number of the miners agreeing to this, had large quantities of their gold coined in five dollar and one dollar pieces, and probably two and a half dollar pieces, with the name of "C Bechtler, Rutherford County, N. C." on one face, on the reverse, the value, the number of grains and carats fine. To give some idea of the amount of gold fluxed and coined by Mr. Bechtler. On one occasion I was in his laboratory where he was working, and noticed the construction of the floor, an ordinary tongued and grooved floor, crossed at right angles, with strips about 2-1/2 inches wide, slightly raised above the main floor, I asked him what was the object of the double floor. In broken English, he said a great many times, be as careful as he could, fine particles of gold would escape, when he was weighing, melting and coining; and so many persons coming in and going out on a smooth floor would carry the scattered gold off; but rubbing their shoes on the slats, the gold would fall between. I asked him if he had ever taken the floor up. The reply was, "Yes, two years after it was laid, and I got two thousand pennyweights of gold." Mr. Bechtler was reported to the treasurer of the United States as violating the constitution. A five dollar Bechtler was sent to the mint, weighed and analyzed, and pronounced all right, and as it did not purport to be the coin of any nation, the government agreed to treat it as bullion. After the death of Christopher, Sr., his nephew, Christopher Bechtler, Jr., continued for several years to smelt, coin and analyze gold. These coins are rapidly disappearing, the great bulk of them having been recovered or converted into jewelry, those still extant being a premium.

The gold of this county is usually found in rather small particles, a nugget of any size was rarely found. I don't remember but two that weighed as much as five ounces. The first was found at the Corpening mine about four miles north-east from Morganton, the second on the Fleming mine, on a branch of Lower creek some time after the late war. A nugget partially crystalized found at the latter, is now in my possession, weighing a little less than four ounces. It is the most brilliant and beautiful specimen of virgin gold I ever saw.

Dr. Horace B. Satterwhite, who was engaged in mining in this county, had a theory that gold grew like other things, in nature, and was the production of a chemical process constantly going on, which gave rise to a chemist's fruitless attempts to discover "The Philosopher's Stone." The Doctor said this was proven by the fact that the old mines were profitably worked over so often. Professor Frederic Overman, a distinguished mining engineer and scientist, explains satisfactorily I think, the increase or the growing as the Doctor called it. In a book published by him in 1851, he says:

"There are localities in the gold region of the Southern States, where every piece of rock, and every handful of soil contains more or less of the precious metal. The primary source of this metal, is evidently in granite or its associate rocks; and it is from the abrasion of these rocks and when the gold is in an alluvial deposit and found in a stream, it is an indication of there being no vein." He further says that "veins by infiltration from the surface, do not extend to any great depth bearing gold, as contrasted with pyritic veins; pyritics and all other sulphurets of metals, are injected from below, these cannot crystallize from a watery solution, these sulphurets have been driven into crevices of the rocks, either in the form of a vapor, which is most probable, or have been injected in masses by pressure from below; it may be asserted as a fact that all native sulphurets, particularly all of iron contain gold; it does not follow from this, that all pyrites contain sufficient gold to pay for its extraction; as sulphurets cannot possibly penetrate any rock but from below, we naturally conclude that the heaviest body of such kind of ore must necessarily lie deep in the earth. This conclusion is supported and confirmed by practice, for all pyriteous veins are invariably found to improve in quality and quantity with the depths. This circumstance speaks very favorably for the gold formation of the Southern States. We have here a belt of gold ores of unparalleled extent, immense width and undoubtedly reaching the primitive rock which, on an average, cannot be less than 3,000 feet deep; here in a mass of precious metal, enclosed in the rock, that cannot be extracted for ages, and in this respect the region in question is the most important of all the known gold deposits, California not excepted."

I have given these extended opinions of an expert, distinguished in matters pertaining to the origin, formation and permanence of gold veins, and more particularly of what he says of pyritic or sulphuret veins, to encourage those who may own them in gold regions and may happen to see this writing. The failure of miners hitherto in realizing a profit from this species of vein, although found to be rich in gold at and near the surface, which by long exposure to atmospheric action had dispelled the sulphurets and set the gold free, but soon by going down on the vein the sulphurets became solid and the gold imperceptible, and owing to the great expense attending the reduction of the gold by chemical process until recently (as I learn) it can now be done at a comparatively small expense. I know of several large veins of this character in Burke, Caldwell and Rutherford. Some of them have been partially worked, and abandoned on account of the increase of the sulphurets.

Gold working in this and adjoining counties for years was confined to lowlands on the creeks and branches, and at first, gold was taken from a strata of alluvial sand and gravel by a very simple and primitive process, using a shallow iron pan, holding about three quarts. When this vessel is filled with alluvial sand and gravel, immersed in water, stirred with the hand and frequently shaken, the gold sinks to the bottom, and the sand, clay and gravel flow off with the water, or are taken out by the hand. This was the mode of operation at the first. Afterward, some one invented a very original and simple machine called a Teemer: A wooden box about 2½ feet long, 18 inches wide, with a hopper at one end inserted for the reception, and a spout at the other for the escape of the sand and gravel. A trough square, made of plank, 2 feet in width and 6 feet long, placed about 3 feet above the mouth of the machine with an inclination of a degree or so, that the water would run rapidly with force so as to carry the gravel and sand thrown into the trough from a pit by one of the operators. Another standing at the lower end received the gravel and sand in a rudely constructed seive, and by constantly shaking it, separated the large gravel from the sand, preventing the clogging of the Teemer. After running the machine for some time they would stop. The water in the trough becoming clear, they would pick up by hand the sparkling nuggets and large particles of gold left in the trough. At sunset, the gold in the Teemer was secured by washing with a pan the remaining sand. No quicksilver was used, and the appearance of the metal was much more brilliant and beautiful. Then, when amalgamated by the slow mode, I have witnessed as much as 50 pennyweights taken from a mine of my father's on a small stream near the Rocky Ford of the Catawba, within less than 3 miles from Morganton. Many thousands of pennyweights of the precious metal have been found, and occasionally now nuggets are picked up within one-fourth of a mile of the town. No doubt there are still undiscovered rich placer mines in this region of gold. It has been found in the South Mountains, 3,000 feet above sea level.

BURKE'S OLD SHERIFFS

William Morrison was the first sheriff of this county, was either Scotch or of Irish descent, and owned a plantation on Muddy Creek. He was a soldier of the Revolution, was a leading citizen of his day, a member of the Legislature in 1779. His son, Frank Morrison, I remember in 1827. He resided at the old homestead on Muddy creek, which is still in the possession of his descendants. He was a man highly esteemed by all who knew him, of fine physique, a worthy scion of a patriotic, popular ancestor.

Peter Mull was elected sheriff in 1790.

Thomas McEntire was the second sheriff about 1790? Emigrated from Tyrone county, Ireland, at the same time as James McEntire, Sr., shortly after the Revolution, was a near relative, probably a nephew. He resided near Old Fort, now in McDowell County, was a member of the Legislature in 1802, had three sons and two daughters, James, William and John, Jennie and Mary. Some years after the decease of their father, the sons removed to Georgia. Jennie married Thomas Lytle, and lived at the old homestead until their decease. Mary married David Greenlee, one of the sons of James Greenlee, Sr. The issue of this marriage was two sons, James and Thomas Young, and two daughters, Mary and Martha. James' first wife was a daughter of a Mr. Morris, of Rutherford county, by whom he had a son, David, who now lives on the fine plantation owned by his grandfather in McDowell county. Thomas Y. married the daughter and only child of Robert Logan, one of the first and most skilled land surveyors of the county. Mr. T. Greenlee is still living on the plantation inherited by his wife from her father. Mary married James H. Greenlee, Esq., of Turkey Cove, by whom he has two sons. Martha married John H. Greenlee, son of Ephriam Greenlee, Sr., no issue. The Greenlees came originally from Virginia, and were among the wealthiest of the old pioneers of Burke.

Hugh Tate, third sheriff in 1803, was a descendant of "Rock" Samuel Tate, who was the ancestor of the Tates of Burke, and Pennsylvania. He emigrated from Ireland, previous to the Revolution or shortly thereafter. Sheriff Hugh Tate married Margaret, a daughter of Alexander Erwin, a sister of Col. James Erwin. He had issue two sons and one daughter. The late Doctors, Samuel and William C. Tate. Samuel married his cousin, Elizabeth, of Pennsylvania, by whom he had issue Wistar, Robert, Lucius, Hugh Al. and Julia (four sons and one daughter.) William C. Tate married Mrs. Laura Polk, nee Wilson relict of Marshall Polk, Sr., by whom he had issue three sons and three daughters, Joseph, Hugh and Knox, Emma, Catherine [Mrs. W. E. Powe] and Laura [Mrs. J. A. Young mother of Mary Young—Gaither.] The Tates were leading men of note and distinction in their day. Eliza, daughter of Sheriff Hugh, married her cousin, Col. Samuel C. Tate, by whom he had one son and a daughter, the late Captain Junius C. Tate, and Mary J.

Hodge Rabourne. Hodge Rabourne, fourth sheriff, 1810, after Hugh Tate, was a popular man as evinced by his election to the Legislature, in the commons with Alexander Erwin in 1804 and in the Senate 1812 and 1813. Of his ancestors, antecedents, or descendants I know nothing.

NOTE: Eston (Athan) McDowell was sheriff of Burke county in 1815 as is shown by records in office of Seat of State at Raleigh.   **WCE**

Mark Brittain. Mark Brittain, fifth sheriff after Rabourne, 1817, of him see sketch, page 59.

Samuel McD. Tate, Sr. Samuel McD. Tate, Sr., sixth sheriff, successor of Brittain, 1827, second son of David Tate, Sr., a bachelor, never married.

William C. Butler. William C. Butler, seventh sheriff, 1830. Married Margaret, a daughter of William Tate, Sr., of Hickory Grove, former residence of John Bowman, by whom he had one daughter, Sarah. She married the late E. E. Greenlee, of Tennessee.

Col. Samul C. Tate. Col. Samuel C. Tate, eighth sheriff, successor of W. C. Butler, about 1834, son of William Tate, Sr., a man of sterling worth and character, a grandson of the patriotic soldier, John Bowman, as before stated, killed at the battle of Ramsaur's Mill. Col. Tate died in the prime of life at Hickory Grove.

John Boone. John Boone, ninth sheriff, 1835, had a warm contest with F. P. Glass, Esq. Both men were popular. Boone was elected by a small majority. John Boone was a near relative [great nephew] of the celebrated pioneer and distinguished hunter, Daniel Boone, who was born and lived until mature manhood in the valley of the Yadkin river. His name and fame has become historical and perpetual. The county town of Watauga being named for him, and also in the splendid Rotunda of the magnificent marble capital of the United States. Amid other scenes of daring and prowess of the early history of the nation, is a prominent one of life size, representing Boone in hunter's costume, engaged in deadly contest with two stalwart Indian warriors, one lies breathing his last with the hero's right foot placed upon his breast, his right arm raised in the act of plunging his knife in the breast of his startled foe.

A tradition. said to be a fact, of how Boone wooed and won his wife, (Isabella Kincaid) may be of interest to my readers. On one occasion, while hunting deer in his canoe by firelight on the upper waters of the Yadkin river, approaching the margin of stream, he saw (or thought so), by the gleaming light of his torch, the eyes of a deer reflected. Raising his rifle to shoot, a woman screamed and fled with the speed of a frightened doe. Leaving his canoe he followed the footsteps of the fugitive until she took refuge in her home. Entering the house, Boone apologized for the fright he had given her. She forgave him and sealed it with hand and heart.

John H. Pearson. John H. Pearson, successor to John Boone, 1836. son of Isaac Pearson, of Silver Creek, was the tenth sheriff of Burke, a man as is well known to many now living, kind, hospitable, of unswerving integrity and honesty in all his dealings with his fellow man, and in the discharge of all his duties as a county officer, of great popularity, so much so, that I do not remember that he ever had any opponent for the office of sheriff, holding it for as long as he desired it. In his time as sheriff and until the penitentiary was established in 1848 or 1849, the whipping post and pillory were still used for the punishment of crimes except homicides, burglaries, arson, etc. Delaware, I believe, is the only State in the Union that has not abolished the whipping post. I know that it is regarded by any intelligent person as a relic of barbarism, and strange to say, there are others who regard hanging for murder as equally so. The object of our criminal laws, as I understand them, is to punish and humiliate those who violate them, not only to suppress, but to deter others, and thus degrading them visit the "sins of the fathers upon the children." It seems to me that the penitentiary in this State has in a great measure, failed to acccomplish what it was designed to do, hence we see men, white and black, who had served the time of their sentence, returning and mingling among the people and received as though they had never been degraded by their crimes, or the wearing of the striped clothes of the convicts. What effect does it have on the colored population if one of their number is sent to the State prison for stealing a chicken or watermelon?

So far as I see and observe there is no difference made between those of them who have established a character for honesty, and those who have been convicted and served a term in the penitentiary, and wore for a time its stigma. Although there is but little hope for the restoration of the whipping-post, yet for one I favor it, and believe from the conversations which I have had with the better class of white people as well as black, a majority would vote for it if the question was submitted. There are comparatively few living now who witnessed its good and lasting effects. The man that had his bare back exposed to the public gaze and was beaten with many stripes that could not be obliterated, was degraded during life. The mark of Cain was fixed upon him, and his posterity.

I never knew but one man in this county who, by his manner and action, did not regard this public punishment as degrading. A man had been convicted of larceny under such circumstances that the presiding judge sentenced him to a double punishment, being twice that usually inflicted, 39 lashes at the public whipping post instanter, and 39 lashes to be repeated 30 days thereafter. This was done by Sheriff Pearson. A large crowd followed the sheriff and culprit to the place of punishment near the present jail. The man's clothing was stripped to the small of the back, so as to leave that portion of the back above bare, his hands and wrists were pinioned in iron clamps on each side of the large post, so that he hugged it. The switches used were hickory of one year growth, seasoned, prepared for the purpose. At each blow of the rod the sufferer made a suppressed appeal to the sheriff, every stroke cut the tender skin, and made a mark indelible. After the required number of lashes had been given, and his clothing adjusted, he faced the crowd who had evidently by word and looks, sympathized with the wretch while he was being punished. With a smile he said: "Gentlemen and ladies, I thank you for your attention on this occasion, and shall be happy to see you thirty days from this time, when I will again make my appearance on this platform." This peroration was greeted with loud applause by the assembled crowd.

THE NECROMANCER

I remember an amusing incident told me by my uncle, Thomas L. McEntire, that occurred in the old Tate Hotel(a), where a numerous collection of the olden residents of Morganton indulged in a hearty laughter at their own expense and gullibility.

A stranger had advertised that he was endowed with a supernatural gift, by which he could make himself both visible and invisible in the presence of all who would honor him with their attendance in the large reception hall of the hotel, performance to begin sharp at nine o'clock p.m., admission 12-1/2 cents, children half price. The wizard himself received the admission fee at the front entrance. A small table brilliantly lighted with candles stood at the rear side of the hall; a curtain was hung near, but behind the table coming from behind the curtain with outstretched arms and upturned eyes, in a low sepulchral voice, he said: "Fellow mortals, you now see that I am visible; in a short time I will become invisible." After waiting for sometime to witness the invisible part of the programme, the audience became impatient, evinced by hissing, stamping, whistling, and calling aloud. McEntire, who was something of a wag, said: "I expect the wizard has redeemed his pledge." Walking to the table, he drew the curtain aside. The back door of the room, which had been masked by the curtain, was open and the bird of passage had flown to parts unknown. The applause was long and loud, laughter and enjoyment reigned, and there was not even a suggestion that the wizard was a swindler.

THE FIRE KING

In the same hall more than sixty years since, I witnessed with many others contemporaneous, an exhibition most wonderful, by a man calling himself a "Fire King", which seemed almost miraculous, and no doubt if it had taken place in Italy as late even as the sixteenth century, he would have been arrested and tried by the inquisition for a compact with the devil and put to death. I am not sure, but some of those who witnessed his insivible feats with fire believed that he was a confederate with his "Satanic Magesty", otherwise how could he with impunity so handle and drink those burning, boiling substances. His hands, mouth, throat and stomach were apparently perfectly callous to

---

(a) One of the first large buildings was built in Morganton in 1792 by John Tate on the northwest corner of Union and Greene streets. When he moved to Ga. this house was turned over to his brother, David and called the Tate Hotel. David later built a home and store on the northwest corner of Union and Sterling.

the known effects of fire. For instance, taking a piece of flaming pine from the fire, after the flame had ceased, he would bite off the red hot coals and spit them out, after cooling in his mouth. He said any one of the spectators could do this, under his instruction, provided they had the courage to try it, and he would pay a forfeit if any injury followed. There was a negro present by name Jim Collins, a full blooded African (and by way of digression, it is known that they are much less afraid of fire than the whites and rarely complain of heat. I owned a negro African woman, who rarely in warm weather wore anything on the head as a protection from heat, a very hot day in summer she was binding wheat, with sweat pouring from her face, I said: "Sarah, why don't you put something on your head to protect it from the heat of the sun?" "Why master," was the reply, "I have never seen the day that was too hot for me.")

Jim presented himself and said: "I am willing, you may try it on me." After saying something to Jim, which I did not hear, he lighted a stick of sealing wax. Jim protruded his long tongue, and the blazing wax was dropped deliberately upon it, cooling upon the tongue. He was asked if it burnt him, and he said, "No." The king then melted a quantity of lead in a ladle. Passing by the audience, he in small portions scooped up the melted lead with his fingers, putting it in his mouth, you could hear it hiss as it cooled, placing the pellets as cooled in the hands of the spectators. Heating Florence oil over a spirit lamp in a large spoon so hot that it scorched and burnt a feather, brought almost if not quite to the boiling degree, he supped and swallowed it as if it had been soup of ordinary temperature, with other similar feats extraordinary.

EARLY SCHOOLS OF BURKE

The schools of Burke County of which I write were previous to the enactment by the Legislature of a law appropriating the annual income of the Literary fund among the several counties of the State, on the ratio of the federal population, for the establishment and support of common schools about 1830, which did not become effective for many years after the passage of the act. The teachers of the schools previous to this were invariably employed by the parents or guardians of the pupils at a salary agreed upon, or so much per capita. After the building of the old brick academy by subscription of the citizens in 1823 or 4, on the site now owned by Major J. W. Wilson, and where his residence is erected, trustees were appointed and the tutors for a time selected by them.

The first school that I have any information of was taught by the Rev. John L. Davis about 1815. My brother, John A. Walton, was a pupil of his. I have in my possession an old manuscript in the form of a pamphlet. The figures in the integers, sums, etc., are his; the rules, examples and headings, such as addition, multiplication, reductions, etc., in the handwriting of Mr. Davis. The dates given are from the 1st of March, 1817, to the 2nd of February, 1818. A number of the sums worked, as well as examples, is the reduction of English sterling pounds, shillings and pence to dollars and cents. This occurred in an age when a very strict discipline was observed and maintained, and the rules adopted by the master were imperative, and woe to the culprit who disregarded any of them. The tyrant master was greatly feared, sitting in his curule chair, rod in hand, with frowning wrinkles of the brow.

"His front yet threatens, and his frowns command," while the awe-striken urchins cower under his gaze like chickens when the hawk soars above them. As an illustration, in the handwriting of the pedagogue, are these lines: "John A. Walton, you are a bad boy; you must rule your lines straight; if you do not I shall use the rod. June the 6th, 1817." No doubt the proverb of Solomon had its influence and the rod was spared.

Mr. Davis I remember in 1823. He was very deeply pockmarked, his face corrugated with wrinkles like a washing board, and his sandy-colored hair stood erect like "Old Hickory's." Six feet in height, gaunt and ungainly in form, take him all in all as he stood, he was the ugliest man I ever saw with one exception (of him hereafter). Mr. Davis, however, was much esteemed by his neighbors; he was entry taker of the county in 1820. He was also a preacher in what was then called a meeting house, free of all denominations, now the handsomely improved and enlarged Presbyterian church. I have heard Methodists, Quakers, Socinians and Episcopalians, all preach and hold religious services in the old church. It was the only building in Morganton for the public worship for many years. Mr. Davis was either a Socinian or Unitarian in religious belief. Arithmetical books seem to have been scarce in Mr. Davis' time, as evinced by his mode of instruction. Judging from the manuscript in my possession, he invented or concocted all the rules, examples, etc., in the manuscript and wrote them with his own hand for the instruction of his pupils. As a further proof of the want of such books, about this time a man by the name of Conway, an Irishman by birth, who had been well educated, and who was a talented mathematician, proposed to the merchants and other good citizens of the county interested in education of their children, to write, have printed and bound an arithmetic by subscription, a certain number of copies at so much a copy. The copyright to be retained exclusively by him. The manuscript submitted to the subscribers, was approved, the book was printed and used in the schools. I have in my possession one of the original copies, in a good state of preservation (except the loss of the title page and a few leaves) which I prize as a relic used by members of my own family three-quarters of a century since. The book itself, I think, proves its author to have been one of no little mathematical talent. One or two extracts from the book will probably be interesting to the descendants of those who aided in its publication. The old merchants after the Revolution, in the different States, kept their accounts in pounds, shillings and pence, not English sterling, but what was termed currency, differing in value in some of the states in the Union. The following table is given for the information of the pupil to enable him to make the proper calculation to ascertain the worth of a pound in each State according to its currency in dollars and cents:

Table of the currency in each State

States	Amt. per dollar		Am't pd	
	S.	D.		
New England	6	0	3	33-1/3
Virginia	"	"		"
Kentucky	"	"		"
Tennessee	"	"		"
Pennsylvania	7	6	2	66-2/3
Maryland	"	"		"
New Jersey	"	"		"
New York	7	0	2	50
North Carolina	"	"		"
South Carolina	4	8	4	28-1/2
Georgia	"	"		"

Rule follows

To change New England, Virginia, Kentucky and Tennessee currency into that of New York and North Carolina currency, which is at 8 shillings per dollar, as the currency of the New England, Virginia, Kentucky and Tennessee States is at 6 shillings per dollar, add one third to the same and the answer will be in New York and North Carolina currency, which is at 8 shillings per dollar—this under the head of domestice exchange.

There is also a table of interest occupying several pages of the arithmetic, from one dollar to one thousand, calculated at 6 per cent from one month to five years. Under the rule of fellowship, he gives the following example, giving the names of four of the leading merchants of Morganton in 1818: Four merchants of Morganton, Erwin & Company, John Caldwell, Thomas Walton, and Samuel Newland sent to Charleston for a load of goods which amounted to 8,000 dollars. A hogshead of wine comprising part of the load was staved, by which they sustained a loss of 100 dollars. However, the rest of the goods arrived, and which they immediately sold for 10,000 dollars. What was the respective portion of the gain on the goods?

$10,000 selling price
8,000 prime cost
_____
$ 2,000
100 wine lost
_____
$ 1,900 net gain

If 8,000; 1,900: 3,000: Erwin & Co.'s gain $ 712.50

If 8,000: 1,900: 2,000: Jno. Caldwell's gain   475.00
If 8,000: 1,900: 1,500: Thos. Walton's gain   356.25
If 8,000: 1,900: 1,500: Sam'l Newland's gain   356.25
                                                                                              ———————
                                           Proof $1,900.00

Compound Multiplication: Example.
                                                                   Morganton. Nov. 12, 1818
David Tate, Esq.,
                Bought of Erwin & Co.
25 pounds of sugar at — S   D
                                   2   4 1/2 per pound
37 pounds of coffee
                    at   3   6   per pound
13 yards of calico at   3   9   per yard   L   S   D
                                                                          ————————————————
                                           Total   11   17.7   1/2

Under the head of "Pleasant and Diverting Questions", among
many others, is the following:

> "A lady was asked her age; who replied thus
> 'My age if multiplied by three,
> Two-sevenths of that product, tripled be,
> The square root, of two-ninths of that is four;
> Now tell me my age or never see me more.' "

If a problem like the above, was submitted to some of the young
gallants of Morganton by a young lady of whom he had the temerity
to ask her age, would find some difficulty, if not insuperable in solv-
ing the problem. Mr. Conway, like a great many of old Erin's sons,
indulged very freely in Potteen, which finally resulted in his being
drowned in Col. W. W. Erwin's mill pond.

Mr. Davis' successor was Rev. Mr. Eddy, about 1824 or 1825, a
Presbyterian minister. He came with his wife and a maiden lady named Gould. They were people of culture, highly educated. They were
the first to teach in the newly erected brick academy, the children,
male and female, conjointly of the leading citizens at that time. For
some cause, I know not, Mr. Eddy and family did not remain long. As
I remember Mr. Alexander Wilson succeeded Mr. Eddy as an instructor or tutor. His father, Rev. McCamy [McKamie] Wilson, married a
daughter of Alexander Erwin, Sr., and thus his children were relatives
of both branches of the old Erwins, of Burke county. Mr. Alexander
Wilson was named for his maternal grandfather, and was much esteemed on account of his highly moral character as well as his capacity
as an instructor. I do not know of one person now living (excepting
probably James H. Greenlee, of Turkey Cove, McDowell County)
that was a pupil of either Mr. Eddy or Wilson, and soon alas? unless

some more enduring mode than that which I have adopted by publication in a newspaper, these crude reminiscences of "Auld Lang Syne" of Burke county, and its pioneers, calling to the notice of their descendants and others, some marked characteristics of the virtues, patriotism, peculiarities, anecdotes, etc., will soon pass away and be forgotten like a fitful dream of the past.

Succeeding Mr. [John McKamie] Wilson as tutors, were two brothers, natives of this county, Lee and Clinton Owens, who taught the younger and less advanced pupils in one of the rooms of the academy, while the Rev. John Silliman, a Presbyterian minister, instructed the more advanced in the Greek and Latin languages. Mr. Silliman was a native of Virginia. Among the number of young men who studied the classics under him were Alphonso, Edward Jr., and Alexander Hamilton, sons of Col. W. W. Erwin; Joseph J. and W. C. Erwin, sons of Col. James Erwin; James H. Tate, son of David Tate, Sr.; Robert Baird, son of Matthew Baird; Burgess S. Gaither, Robert C. Pearson, James H. Greenlee, and John A. Walton, Mr. Silliman at first occupied the Presbyterian parsonage for a number of years, but finally purchased a farm on Silver creek, about six miles west of Morganton, and moved to it. Mr. Silliman was very successful in gathering a large congregation in this neighborhood, many of the best and most influential farmers becoming communicants of the Presbyterian church. Among them were the Corpenings, O'Neals, Nails, McElraths, Londons, Pearsons, Hemphills, Morrisons and others. Religious services were held in a substantial, hewed log building, fitted up with glazed windows and pews, and was known as the Silver Creek Meeting House. Nearby was established a camp-ground, where as late as 1837, the best as well as the wealthiest citizens of the county, living within 8 miles of the site, erected log cabins, used as tents, and religious services were held annually for three or four days. Large crowds assembled, hospitality was unstinted, everybody was welcomed and fed on the fat of the land. It was verily an annual jubilee, which all seemed to enjoy. This was the only Presbyterian campground I ever knew in Burke. Although Mr. Silliman lived six miles from Morganton, he continued his ministration at that point. This good man was much beloved by all who knew him. In some respects he was like St. Paul, he was noted for his long sermons, and although I never knew any to be like Eutychus so overcome by their slumbers as to fall from their seats, yet, not infrequently, I saw some of the shining lights making with shut eyes, low bows to the preacher at intervals. Near Captain Charles McDowell's home, Quaker Meadows, about 1834, a school was taught by Thomas Hill that had a good reputation, being well sustained and patronized by the McDowells, Averys, Erwins and others. Some of their sons were well prepared by Mr. Hill for entering the University of the State. For a time succeeding Mr. Hill, William Lavender, a relative of the Averys and [brother of] the wife of Joseph Perkins, a man eccentric, witty, something of a poet, lampooned the young gallants of the time (myself among the number) in doggerel rhymes and meter, after "John Gilpin style" on their unsuccessful efforts to win an encouraging smile from the fair ones, by whom they were enamoured. These and other ludicrous rhymes were distributed by the author in the neighborhood for the amusement of young and old.

FALLING METEORS

Reading recently in a religious periodical that on the 15th of November, 1899, the path of the earth in its orbit will take it through a particular swarm of meteorites called the Leonides (which travel around the sun in about thirty-three years) which will give to the inhabitants on this terestrial globe then living a celestial pyrotechnic exhibition far exceeding anything heretofore "visible to the existing generation of men," this article called to my recollection the resplendent shower of meteorites in November, 1833; such a magnificent display of falling stars (as many thought) has never been witnessed by the oldest persons of that generation, and many of them, awe stricken, believed that the apocalytic vision of St. John was being fulfilled, the stars of heaven were falling, and the heaven would depart as a scroll, when "it is rolled together." A man by the name of Scott was walking through the streets of Morganton reading from the Bible the prophetic vision. The colored population was almost frantic with fear. An amusing episode told me by Col. Avery, occurred at "Swan Ponds." Among his numerous slaves was a faithful servant named Jacob, a foreman in whom the colonel placed great confidence, so if anything wrong or unusual occurred at night he would speedily notify his master. During the meteoric shower Col. Avery was awakened by a loud and rapid knocking at the door. Springing from his bed, alarmed, he said to his wife, "That is Jake, something unusual has occurred." Opening the door, he said, "What is the matter?" "Oh, Lord, master, Judgment Day has come, the stars are nearly all down." "Oh, no Jake", said Colonel Avery, "those fiery flakes are not stars, they are meteors. You look at the seven stars and see if you miss any of them." Jake replying said, "I can't count but six, masser."

OLD-TIME PREACHERS

Methodist preachers whom I knew in my youth and early manhood, and whose ministrations were local, being almost exclusively confined to Burke county, covering the original boundary of 1777, vis.: Reverend William Fullwood, distinguished as "Father Fullwood", born 1763, joined the conference in 1792, professed sanctification sixteen years before his death. Richard Bird joined the conference at the same time as Father Fullwood. Following them were Jeremiah Stacey, James Stacey, and later Thomas and John Dorsey and others. These were all devout men of the Methodist ministry, of unblemished character, very zealous and largely instrumental and successful in spreading the Gospel according to the doctrines of their celebrated founder, the Rev. John Wesley. The buildings in which these good men preached and held their religious services were called meeting houses, and were almost invariably called after the sacred places of the Old Testament, such as Bethel, Nebo, Sardis, Gilboa, Salem, etc. The buildings were of plain architecture and material. No ornamentation, no music except congregational singing, and the sermons and prayers were extemporaneous. There was but one place for public worship in Morganton until the Episcopal Church was erected in 1845, and the Methodist in 1846, and now its membership is by far the largest in the prosperous town of Morganton. Immense crowds attended the old annual camp meetings in the county and great religious excitement prevailed. The surrounding woods resounded with the shouts of the converted and hundreds of voices joined in the time-honored hymn of redemption:

> "The year of jubilee is come;
> The year of jubilee is come;
> Return ye ransomed sinners home."

The old time camp meetings that caused so much religious fervor, have become almost obsolete. Some of these old preachers were severe on the "pomps and vanities of the wicked world", the wearing of gaudy apparel, jewels, the braiding of the hair, etc. I was present many years since at the Salem meeting house when a large congregation had gathered. The preacher was distinguished somewhat, for being personal when he thought it necessary for the spiritual welfare of his audience. He prefaced his sermon (after looking over the congregation) as follows:

"It is a very foolish and remarkable fact that some people are not satisfied with the way that God Almighty has made them; here are white people who have naturally straight hair, that they are trying to make curl, while on the contrary, the negroes have naturally curly hair are trying by twisting, pulling and binding it with strings to make it straight."

Whether this home thrust had the desired effect, I know not; but certainly some faces were lighted up with broad smiles, while others of the fair sex, amenable to the rebuke, blushed with confusion.

Temperance societies before 1840 were not organized in this county, although drunkeness and excessive use of ardent spirits were denounced by the preachers as a great sin, quoting St. Paul as saying that "No drunkard should inherit the Kingdom of Heaven." They did not however, object to drinking wine in moderation, perhaps remembering the same apostle's injunction to Timothy: "Drink no longer water but use a little wine for thy stomach's sake." Until the celebrated temperance lecturer, Philip S. White, came to the county and lectured in the court house in 1849, the good people of Burke did not have much faith in the efficacy of temperance societies for the cure of habitual drunkards, and time has proven that other remedies beside moral suasion in most cases had to be resorted to. As far back as 1830, I remember an instance of a man who was permanently cured by a remedy given him by my father. His name was Elisha Coxe, a well-to-do farmer living near the base of the Blue Ridge, in what is now McDowell county, a very respectable, good citizen, a friend and customer of my father. When attending the courts at Morganton he would invariably get drunk and involved himself in trouble. My father being in Charleston, S. ,C., purchasing goods, heard that a sure remedy for the cure of drunkenness had been discovered and was for sale at a drug store. It was called "Chamber's Mixture", and he purchased a quart bottle of it. Shortly afterwards, coming to court, Coxe walked into the store, and after shaking hands, my father said: "Coxe, I have some good whiskey, won't you have a drink?" "Oh, you are joking squire", said Coxe. "You are the last man that would ask me to drink liquor." "No, Coxe", my father replied, "I am in earnest. I thought of you while in Charleston, and some others of my friends, and brought it for the express purpose of giving you a drink." A glass and the mixture was placed upon the counter. There were directions that it to be given in small doses three times. Walton was in a dilemma. If he poured out the small dose, he thought Coxe would take it as an insult and refuse to drink, resulting, of course, in Coxe's pouring out a big draught and swallowing it. Smacking his lips, with thanks, he said it was first rate. As all is not gold that glitters, so all may not be unadulterated whiskey that smells and tastes like it. This fact Coxe soon realized. He became deathly pale and sick, and reeled so that he could scarce keep his feet. My father, alarmed, had him taken into the adjoining counting room and put to bed. After much groaning, retching and profuse vomiting, he was in some measure relieved. Finally he arose, and speaking to no one, mounted his horse and went home. About 12 months after he walked into the store. My father expecting that he had come to abuse him for having tricked him, called out, "Hello, Coxe, is that you?" "Yes, sir, and I have come to return you my thanks for the greatest kindness one man ever did for another. By that drink you gave me I have become a sober man. I detest liquor. If I merely smell it my stomach revolts."

It was during the session of the Legislature of 1850-51 that Philip S. White, the great temperance orator, was advertised to deliver a lecture on temperance in the Presbyterian church of Raleigh. The members of the Legislature were invited to attend. the large audience filled the church, composed in part of the elite of the city. Dr. Lacy, the pastor, was seated by the lecturer. Mr. White prefaced his lecture by saying Dr. Lacy had kindly permitted him to deliver his lecture in the church, and "he desired and hoped that there would be no laughing, applause or unseemly conduct in this sacred place", well knowing at the time that his eloquence and anecdotes would render his request negatory. At intervals, in the course of his long lecture, applause and laughter was loud and long prolonged. After a subsidence of the din, the speaker's manner and voice changed. In a deep-tond, organ-like voice, he said: "Fellow mortals, I would be willing to risk my reputation and all my worldly goods of the truth, that every tenth man in this large assemblage will fill a drunkard's grave." John Hayes, a member from of the Legislature from Caldwell, facetious and witty, six feet in stature, thin and boney in structure, with face and hard features like "Old Hickory's," wrapped in an old fashioned camlet cloak that reached to his ankles, and looking as solemn as a judge, when in the act of pronouncing a death sentence on a criminal, rose and said in a clear and shrill voice: "Mr. White, I will bet you a quart of bald face that you have told a lie." Hayes took his seat amid roars of applause and laughter. White seemed dumfounded and the facetious Hayes was the lion of the evening.

COL. DAVID CROCKETT

I do not suppose there is a man living in Burke county (unless he learned the fact from me) that ever knew that David Crocket (who was not surpassed in his day as a mighty hunter) was ever in the town of Morganton. It was after he had been elected from one of the backwoods districts of Tennessee a member of Congress in 1828 or '29. Riding up in front of the old Tate Hotel, he dismounted and hitched his horse to a rack that stood on Union street about 30 feet from the hotel. Hearing that this famous man was in town, a crowd of young men soon gathered around him. While regaling them with hunting tales, sidesplitting jokes and anecdotes of perilous encounters with panthers, bears, etc., his horse became restive and was trying to rid himself of the bridle by rubbing against a post of the rack. In angry tones he cursed the horse, swearing he would kill him if he didn't stop, and picking up a stone, with the unerring skill of an expert, he threw it, striking the animal on the head. It fell as though he had been shot when Crockett said: "There, d. . .n you; I told you I would kill you, and sure enough I have done it." After this characteristic incident the horse, after a slight struggle, got up, and Crockett bade farewell to the young men who had been so highly entertained by him.

I have a small book published sometime before the war with Mexico which gives a graphic description of the life and exploits of Col. Crockett, entitled "Sketches and Eccentricities of Col. Crockett", by an unknown author. From many of his unparallelled hunting exploits I have selected one which may amuse and, perhaps, interest some of those who take an interest in reading these sketches of the olden time:

"Sitting by a good fire in my little cabin on a cool November evening, roasting potatoes and playing with my children, when somebody hollowed at the fence. I went out and there were three strangers who said they came to take an elk hunt. I was glad to see them and invited 'em in, and after supper we cleaned our guns. I took down old

Betsy, rubbed her up, greased her and laid her away to rest. She is a mighty rough old piece, but I love her, for she and I have seen hard times. She mighty seldom tells a lie. If I hold her right she always sends the ball where I tell her. After we were all fixed I told 'em hunting stories till bed time.

"Next morning was clear and cold, and by the time I sounded my horn, and my dogs came howling 'bout me, ready for a chase, Old Rattler was a little lame—a bear bit him in the shoulder; but Soundwell, Tiger and the rest of 'em were all mighty anxious. We got a bite and saddled our horses. I went by to git a neighbor to drive for us, and off we started for the Harricane. My dogs looked mighty wolfish. They kept jumping on one another and made for a fight, for they hadn't had one in two or three days. We were in fine spirits and going 'long through very open woods, when one of the strangers said: "I would give my horse now to see a bear." Said I, "Well, give me your horse", and I pointed to one about three or four hundred yards ahead of us, feeding on acorns. I had been looking at him for some time, but he was so far off I wasn't certain what it was. However, I hardly spoke before we all strained off, and the woods fairly echoed as we harked the dogs on. The old bear didn't want to run, and he never broke till we got most upon him; but then he buckled for it, I tell you. When they overhauled him, he just rared upon his hind legs and he boxed the dogs about at a mighty rate. He hugged old Tiger and another till he dropped 'em nearly lifeless; but the others worried him, and after a while they all come to and give him trouble. They are mighty apt, I tell you, to give a bear trouble before they leave him. 'Twas a mighty pretty fight; 'twould have done one's soul good to see it—just to see how they all rolled about. It was as much as I could do to keep the strangers from shooting him, but I wouldn't let them, for fear they would kill my dogs. After we got tired seeing 'em fight, I went in among 'em and the first time they got him down, I socked my knife into the old bear. We then hung him up, and went on to take our elk hunt. You never 'seed' fellows so delighted as them strangers was. Blow me if they didn't cut more capers jumping about than the old bears. 'Twas a mighty pretty fight, but I b'lieve I seed more fun looking at them than at the bear.

"By the time we got to the Harricane, we were all rested and ready for a drive. My dogs were in a better humor for a fight — had just taken off the wiry edge. So I placed the strangers at the stands through which I thought the elk would pass, sent the driver way up aheads, and I went below. Everything was quiet and I leaned old Betsy gin a tree and I laid down. I s'pose I had been lying there about an hour when I heard old Tiger open. He opened once or twice, and old Rattler give a long howl. The balance joined in, and I knew the elk were up. I jumped up and seized my old rifle. I could hear nothing but one continued roar of all my dogs, coming right towards me. Though I was an old hunter, the music made my hair stand on end. Soon after they first started, I heard one gun go off, and my dogs stopped, but not for long, for they took a little back towards where I had placed the strangers. One of them fired, and they dashed back, and circled round way to my left. I ran down about a quarter mile and I heard my dogs make a bend like they were coming to me. While I was listening I heard the bushes breaking still lower down and started to run there. As I was going 'long I 'seed' two elk burst out of Harricane, 'bout one hundred and thirty yards from me. There was an old buck and doe. I stopped, waited until they got into a clear place, and as the old fellow made a leap, I raised old Bet, pulled trigger and she spoke out. The smoke blinded me and I couldn't see what I did; but as it cleared away, I caught a glimpse of only one going away, so I thought I had the other. I went up and there lay the buck a-kicking. I cut his throat, and by that time Tiger and two of my dogs came up. I thought it singular that all my dogs were not there, and began to think they had killed another. After the dogs had bit him and found out he was dead, old Tiger began to growl and curled himself up between his legs. Every thing had to stand off then, for he wouldn't let the devil himself touch him. I started off to look for the strangers my two dogs following. After getting away a piece, I looked back, and once in a while I could see old Tiger git up and shake the elk, to see if he was dead, and then curl up between his legs again. I found the strangers 'round a doe the driver had killed; and one of them said he was sure he had killed one lower down. I asked him if it had horns. He said he didn't see any. I put the dogs where he said he had shot, and they didn't go far before they halted. I went up, and there lay a fine buck elk; and though his horns were four or five feet long, the fellow who shot him was so scared that he never saw them. We had three elk and a bar; so we managed to get it home; then butchered our game, talked over the hunt, and had a glorious frolic."

Alas! poor Crockett had a heroic but sad ending. He was with Fanning and his men at the fall of the Alamo, in Mexico, when they were all massacred by the brutal Mexicans. Crockett was found dead with a number of dead Mexicans whom he had slain lying at his feet. Did he think at this time of horror, or his own well remembered maxim left to his friends?:

"The maxim I leave to my friends when I am dead:
Be sure you are right then go ahead."

THE BARON MUNCHAUSEN OF OLD BURKE

(Copied from manuscript of Col. Thos. Geo. Walton, owned by Louise Boggs.)

Possibly one of papers first published in Morganton Herald in 1894

JOSEPH DOBSON, the ancestor of Alex and John Dobson, old reputable citizens of this county, was the son of Dr. Dobson, who was probably the original owner of the extensive lowlands on the Catawba River known as the "Swan Ponds." Col. Waightstill Avery removed from Mecklenburg to Burke in 1781, at which time he became possessed of this valuable domain and gave to it the name above.

Jos. Dobson was a deputy surveyor under Robt. Logan in 1821, at a time when Burke County contained a large acreage of vacant land lying in the mountains of the Blue Ridge. He entered a great deal of this land in his own name, making the surveys himself, which was endorsed by the county surveyor, and grants accordingly issued to him by the State. In many instances the calls of the grants were so confused as to make it impossible to locate the land with any degree of certainty; and in many instances this has been a fruitful source of conrtoversy, when the chain of title depended on said grants. It was believed by many persons that the   of the grants had never been surveyed or marked — that he probably made a corner at the beginning and made a plat to correspond with the number of acres to be granted; that in some instances there were no chain bearers. In proof of this assertion I have in my possession a deed to which the names of those purporting to be bearers was not signed by them.

Jos. Dobson in his day was a frequent attendant on the court of Burke, either as witness, plaintiff or defendant, and had a reputation for telling unprecedented yarns. I remember when I was about eight years old witnessing a scene in the old McEntire Hotel at night during a county court in the month of January, gathered around a large fireplace, constructed by my maternal grandfather, James McEntire, after the old Scotch style more than a century ago, holding at one time more than a quarter of a cord of wood, and warming the large reception room thoroughly, bidding defiance to the outdoor discomforts of a freezing, stormy, January night. A crowd of the old citizens from every portion of the then extensive county (reaching to the base and at some points beyond the Blue Ridge) in attendance on the court as jurors, plaintiffs, defendants, and witnesses, many of them taking part in telling marvelous hunting tales and experiences of narrow escape by flood and field. Jos. Dobson was called upon to give his opinion and experience as to the endurable qualities of the different species of timber in the forest when used in the construction of fences, farming implements, etc. He replied that he knew of one kind that would outlast stone (which) produced a great deal of laughter with loud applause, one saying: "I will bet you a treat for the crowd that you have lied as usual, and can't prove what you have said." Dobson took the bet (while his audience no doubt thought the old fox had put his foot on the trap at last) and won it in this way, saying: "I made a crang and axle of black locust for my grindstone and it outlasted two stones." Amid loud applause the bet was paid and the treat was enjoyed.

At this time game abounded, and discussion arose as to what species of dogs was adapted best for the catching of deer, each old Nimrod praising his dogs and declaring that they could bot be excelled. At length Doctor's turn came, and being the last it behooved him to cap the climax or lose his reputation of equaling his prototype, Baron Munchausen. Nothing abashed he said he was at one time the owner of the most remarkable dog for form, speed and bottom that was ever known, and all brought about by an accident. On one occasion, hunting for deer on Table Rock Mountain, near the chimney rocks (these are clearly rock formed on the east side by the wearing of water, leaving in places sharp knife-like edges), a large buck was started. The dog, following with speed, encountered the sharp edge of a rock, which split him open from the point of his nose to the end of his tail. "Following as fast as I could, having heard that flesh would grow again if the severed parts were put together before getting cold, I seized the different parts; but in my hurry I turned two legs up and two down. Holding them in this position they had stuck together. My dog got well, and after that I had no trouble in catching deer, after they were started. My dog would run on two of his legs until they were tired, and then switch over and run on the rested legs; and this was continued until the deer was run down and captured." This closed the contest and the victory was awarded to Dobson.

It is said, and I believe it is so, that some of the peculiarities and traits of character (mentally and physically) will crop out in the third or fourth generation. I know a descendant of Dobson who is gifted in telling yarns, some of which savor of the marvelous. I give the following incident told by him. One of his acquaintances, who was in the late war, was so much overcome with fright at the first battle he was in, that he became dumb, losing his voice entirely. Being discharged he came home and remained dumb, but on attempting to cross a mill pond, which was slick with ice, his feet slipped and he fell headlong into the freezing water, exclaiming as he plunged in: "Good Lord!" His tongue was loosed from that moment and his vocal organs fully restored.

THEY ALL LIKED TODDY

At this period of Burke, when a neighbor visits him, a man was thought to be wanting in hospitality unless he invited him to indulge in a "mint julep," "egg-nog," or some refreshment of which ardent spirits formed a part, and so also, when the ladies, elite of the land, called upon each other, wine and cake was invariably offered, and rarely refused, and the effect of the refreshment was never known in any instance to diminish the natural volubility of their tongues. I hope the ladies who read what I have written will not suppose that old age has made me morose or cynical, for I assure them that even when most men of my age are in "the sear and yellow leaf," the dulcet sweet-toned voice of woman is to me and ever has been like beauty, a joy forever: and I ask them to remember the old saying that (I believe to be true): "A man is as old as he feels; a woman as she looks."

Returning from this digression, I remember when a youth at a time when there was a three or four days' meeting held in the Presbyterian Church (there being at the time no other place of worship in Morganton) a number of the ministers of that denomination were always present at my father's, who was a member, and he with others entertained them, and he invariably invited them to take a toddy of French brandy before dinner, and it was an exception when it was refused. Temperance lecturers and societies were unheard of then, and drunkenness was rare among the better classes, and their children were trained to look upon it as a beastly degradation; like the Lacedemonians somewhat, who "trained up their children to hate drunkenness by bringing a drunken man into their company." But notwithstanding this, I have known in my life as many as six of the better class to die in all the demoniacal horrors of delirium tremens. It is an unpleasant and sad task to call to memory the indescribably terrific suffering of those wretched beings whose awful death I witnessed, and I have only done so with the hope that it may catch the eye of some deluded man or youth, who is walking in this broad road to disgrace and destruction in this world; and finally with a foretaste here of his doom hereafter where the tortured soul dieth not, eternally. St. Paul says, "No drunkard shall inherit the kingdom of Heaven."

CONRAD HILDEBRAND

Conrad Hildebrand, the ancestor of the Hildebrands of Burke, was required by a Committee of Safety formed by the leading men of Rowan County in 1774, to deliver to Christopher Beekman, all the powder and flints in his possession, and for the payment of the same to give an order on the committee, which would be accepted by them. Beekman and Hildebrand were residents of that portion of Rowan, now Burke. Of German lineage, active, influential men of their day, Beekman was secretary of said committee and was the first land surveyor of Burke. I have in my possession the original grant and plot of the James Stringfield land of 500 acres, covering a portion of Morganton. The plot is skillfully and neatly drawn, and the quaint handwriting beautiful. The grant was surveyed by David Vance, deputy surveyor (paternal ancestor of Senator Vance) and countersigned by Christopher Beekman, county surveyor. Hildebrand was a member of the Legislature of 1795 and 1797. Some of his descendants still bear the Christian name of the old patriot, Conrad (pronounced by them Coonrod). All of the name Hildebrand have borne a high character for honesty and integrity, as well as others of Dutch origin in this and the adjoining county of Caldwell.

Fifty-five years ago I was a clerk in my father's store. A man came in and asked for some articles of merchandise on a credit. I said: "You will have to wait until my father comes." At length he came and the customer said to him: "Your son refused to credit me for some goods I want." Turning to me, my father said: "My son, if you know a man to be a Dutchman, hereafter when I am not in the store, give him credit for all he wants. I have been a merchant for 40 years and never had but one Dutchman to cheat me, and that was old Fritz Stevilie."

Hon. James Graham

Hon. James Graham succeeded Samuel P. Carson as representative in Congress from this district and served until 1843, when he was defeated by Hon. Thomas L. Clingman, each claiming to be the better Whig. An address to the voters of Burke, signed by Capt. C. McDowell and myself, advocating and endorsing Clingman's claims and charges against his competitor was distributed in the county. At a discussion at Carson's on Buck Creek Graham criticized and ridiculed the address, saying "among other things" caustically: "Who is Thos. G. Walton? I well know it is not my old friend and well-tried Whig so well known and appreciated by the old men who hear us. He would never approve such a document as this." My father being informed of this, said to me with some exhibition of temper: "When next you sign a paper of any kind, do it in such a manner that people will know it is not my sign manual." I agreed, and changed my signature thereafter from "Thos. G." to T. Geo. Walton.

Mark Brittain

Mark Brittain, and old citizen, and for many years sheriff of the county, was elected to the State Senate in 1831 and 1833. A man of respectable character, esteemed by the people and loved by his neighbors, in some respects he was peculiar. His address and manner showed he had a good measure of self-esteem. I know several anecdotes concerning him, some of them not being proper for "ears polite" of course I must omit. His manner and conversation attracted attention in the Legislature. There was an occurrence in which he and the celebrated wit, Jack Stanly, took a part, that convulsed the members of the Senate, that comes under the prohibited head aforesaid. Being on another occasion asked what county he represented, he replied: "I am the pivot on which the county of Burke revolves." He carried a large hickory cane in honor of "Old Hickory," having been his enthusiastic supporter in 1828. The cane was mounted on a silver head on which was engraved his initials "M. B." On being asked by some member of the Legislature what the initials stood for, he replied "Mountain Boomer, sir."

In 1834, being a candidate for the Senate, he had changed his politics, and was no ardent friend of Mr. Clay. At a gathering of the people to hear the candidate for Congress and State Legislature speak in an orchard in the rear of the old house of Mr. W. Mull, Uncle Mark denounced the Democratic party. W. I. Tate, a son of Mr. Wm. Tate of Hickory Grove, rose to his feet and charged him with being a "turncoat." Unabashed, he coolly replied: "Why, Jefferson, my son. Don't you know: 'While the lamp holds out to burn; The vilest sinner may return.'" Uncle Mark was elected, laid aside the hickory stick, and named his fine clay-bank horse "Henry Clay." His son, Sheriff Joseph Brittain in many ways — popularity, fidelity, manner and honesty in all his dealings whatever with men or in discharge of the duties of his office as sheriff — was like his ancestor.

ROBERT CALDWELL PEARSON

Robert Caldwell Pearson (brother of John H. Pearson, of whom I have written in chapter 11 of these reminiscences) was the oldest son of Isaac Pearson by his wife Elizabeth, and was named for his maternal ancestor, Robert Caldwell of "Cherry Fields." Although we differed in politics, Mr. Pearson was my warm personal friend. In many respects he was a remarkable man, of commanding poise and presence, 6 feet 3 or 4 inches in height. With frame and flesh corresponding he was in presence and address so distinguished from ordinary men that when in New York and other cities he was closely observed by men, and the small boys would follow him to gratify their curiosity. His intellectual capacity comported well with banks, capitalists and railroad financiers. So great was his local reputation for foresight, astute, sagacious judgment, that not a few entrusted him with their funds for investment.

He succeeded my father, and was for many years the popular postmaster and a successful merchant of Morganton. Commencing business at an early age as a clerk in the store of his Uncle John Caldwell (a man of exceptional honesty and uprightness), I have no doubt the youth placed in his care, by precept and example was instilled with all those traits which have led to his own success; and which no doubt were the foundation for the character and success of Mr. Pearson in later life. He was for many years before 1861 the leading magistrate, and in my opinion the best in many respects that Burke County ever had. He had studiously informed himself on the duties of his office, was familiar with all the forms required in their discharge. So great was the reliance placed in the equity and justice of his judgments that an appeal was rarely taken to the county or superior courts. Being well versed in the law in regard to administrators and executors, many persons holding such appointments would resort to him to aid them in making their returns and settlements with the courts, Mr. Pearson obliging them without any consideration.

Always affable and polite, he was without exception the best-tempered man I ever knew. Full of the milk of human kindness, he sympathized with those in distress and rejoiced with the happy, always ready and aiding in suppressing feuds among his neighbors. I remember seeing him part two unfortunate townsmen of the same profession, one with his hand throttling the other, his antagonist attempting to draw a pistol. Seizing them with his brawny hands he lifted them apart like pygmies, until their choler cooled. As a traveling companion he excelled. Being my senior by nine years he treated me more like a son, when journeying North together.

In the month of October, 1865, being excluded by the Assembly Proclamation of President Johnson (which provided that none should avail themselves of it who were worth as much as $20,000), Mr. Pearson proposed that we should write a letter to Dr. Powell (a man whom we had known several years before the War), and solicit his aid in obtaining our pardons for the part we had taken during the War. Dr. P. was at one time a resident of Burke, having married a Miss Rust, a daughter of Wm. B. Rust of Bridgewater. He moved to his native State of Tennessee some years previous to the War, and became the intimate friend of Andrew Johnson. Mr. Pearson had heard that he had an office in Washington under the President, who was very much under his influence. The letter was written in Mr. Pearson's persuasive style, and was immediately responded to by Dr. Powell, recognizing us as old friends, and inviting us to come at once to Washington, and we would receive our pardons. Much encouraged you may be sure no time was lost on reaching Washington (by way of Portsmouth and Baltimore), by my friend's good management, costing our war-depleted pocketbooks nothing for steamboat and railroad fare. After seeing the distinguished senator Tom Couwin (?) and delivering a letter in the care of Mr. Pearson from Gov. Vance, asking him as our old friend to use his influence with the President to get his pardon, we went to the Treasury, in which Dr. Powell had an office. Entering a large room we found a number of officials and clerks, sitting at a long table, busily engaged in writing. Addressing a stout grey-headed man sitting at the head of the table, Mr. P. said:

"Will you, Sir, kindly inform me if Dr. Powell is here?"

"He is not, Sir, but if you will call at the White House about 12 o'clock noon, you will find Dr. Powell."

"Thank you, Sir, then my friend will do the President the honor of calling upon him at that hour."

"No doubt, Sir, the President will feel most highly honored by your doing so."

Instantly the retort came:

"In the language of an old friend of mine, 'the feeling will be *reciprokel*'."

One of them said:

"You caught a Tartar that time, old fellow."

Approaching the White House we saw our friend standing on the portico, waving his hand to us, to our great relief and joy. He welcomed us with the particulars of our pardons, with the great seal of the U. S. affixed, and the signed name of the President added. I doubt if there were ever two individuals, who, under the same conditions, felt more grateful for the prompt act of unrequited kindness.

Returning on our way rejoicing, we stopped for a day in Norfolk. Strolling through the market place, we noticed some extra fine beef. Mr. P. asked where it came from.

"From North Carolina."

"Where did the yam potatoes come from?"

"From North Carolina."

"Where did the ground peas come from?"

"From North Carolina."

"Where did the scuppernong grapes come from?"

"From North Carolina."

To the amusement of the bystanders, he exclaimed excitedly: "Hurrah for old North Carolina; she feeds the Old Dominion!"

Mr. Pearson had acquired a habit (which had become fixed) of going out of his office (which fronted on Union Street) regularly every morning at 10 o'clock, and looking up at the sun would sneeze loudly, so that all living near the public square could hear him; and it was a common saying at the time that "it is 10 o'clock by Squire Pearson's timepiece." Mr. Pearson, like all stout, corpulent men, liked a joke and enjoyed a good, hearty laugh, although sometimes at his own expense. Being in Baltimore he went with one of my sons (living in Baltimore at that time) to the Holiday St. Theatre. The play for the night was the "American Cousins." One of the actors had to be troubled with a sneezing fit. Whenever his time to speak came, his sneezing was not very successful. Mr. P. occupied a conspicuous seat in the first tier above the pit. He said: "Stan, I'll show that fellow how to sneeze." Raising his eyes to the chandelier that lighted the stage he gave three or four of his Burke County sneezes, that not only awakened the echoes of the theatre, but every eye was dirctly toward the prominent figure, giving this lesson in the art of sneezing.* The actors for the time were disconcerted, the performance stopped amid uproarious laughter and loud applause of the audience.

Going from Baltimore to New York, he found the same group of actors playing "American Cousins" again. On the seat with him were two young men. As the playing progressed, one of them said: "Jim, I would give five dollars if the same man who was in Baltimore a few nights since were here when this play was being performed. He was a tremendous, big man. I was sitting near him and while the

---

* *It was said that he took a pinch of snuff to start his sneezing.*

actor was beginning to sneeze he just raised himself out of his seat, and expanding his lungs, expelling the air so violently through his nose, that of all the sonorous, ear-splitting sneezes ever heard, that capped the climax, the play ceasing for the time and the laughter and applause of the assemblage, he was the observed of all observers."

Robert C. Pearson was a man of mark in his day, respected by all, loved by many, discharging all his duties honestly and faithfully. If he ever had a personal enemy it never came within my knowledge. Happily married in early life to Jane Spohronia Tate, a lady who proved to him up until the time of his death a help indeed in all those relations and duties incumbent on a good wife, calculated to add to the happiness and secure the prosperity of the husband she loved. The offspring of this marriage was five sons: Robert, James, Cameron, William and John, and three daughters: Ann Elizabeth, Jane S., and Laura, all living except James. Robert Caldwell Pearson, born Dec. 9, 1807 (died Nov. 18, 1867).

COL. JOHN CARSON

Col. John Carson, one of the wealthy and respected citizens of the county, resided during his long life on the beautiful stream known as Buck Creek, having its source near the crest of the Blue Ridge, and famous for the delicious brook trout that abounds in its pellucid water. Col. Carson was closely connected with the McDowells, his first wife a daughter of "Hunting John" McDowell, his second (Mary Moffett) the widow of Maj. Joseph McDowell of Pleasant Gardens. Of these two wives he had eight children; by the second five sons (Dr. John, Wm. M., Sam'l. P., George, and Logan). These were men in their day, looked up to and highly regarded by their neighbors, sustaining the eminence their ancestors had attained in all the relations of life. Col. Carson was a man of strong common sense, dginified and suave in manner and mien, and of ready wit, not infrequently tinged with sarcasm. An instance illustrating this occurred (which I witnessed), accompanying Mr. Harvey Wilson on his way to marry Miss A. Patton of Asheville with a number of his friends and relations from Morganton. Stopping for the night at the hospitable mansion of Col. Carson, and all being jovial as befitted the occasion, a good part of the night was spent in rather boisterous revelry. The morning after the old gentleman entered the room, and after making a low bow to the assembled guests, he took up the violin (aping the attitude of a country fiddler, Dr. W. C. Tate, our violinist of the previous night), and said: "Dr. Tate, did you ever hear me play on the violin?" "No, Sir, I never did." With emphasis he repeated: "Dr. Tate, did you ever hear me play on the fiddle?" "No, Sir, never in my life." "No, Sir, and you never will," repeated our host, and he left the room abruptly. One can well imagine how the Doctor appreciated the joke. A man passing east on the road, whcih was directly in front of the house on the west bank of the creek, having gone a half mile or more to where the public road crosses the

Catawba River, discovered a number of hogs destroying a field of fine corn. Wheeling his horse he rapidly retraced his course, and with loud voice brought the Colonel to the door. He said: "Colonel, your corn on the river is being ruined by a large number of hogs." "Well, Sir, let them ruin it," was the reply. "I don't suppose it will hurt the hogs."

Dr. John Carson, one of his sons by the second wife, was born with white hair, which was not changed in color at maturity. In connection with this freak of nature, a funny incident happened to Dr. Carson about 1830 going to Charleston, S. C., with a drove of cattle for sale. He met my brother James, a merchant at that time. Being old friends and the only acquaintance in the city, he stopped at the hotel where my brother boarded. The doctor said that he had seen an advertisement that white hair could be permanently dyed, and if so he had come to the conclusion to have his dyed black. Walton told him it was often done. The dyeing was speedily done, his head tied up with a towel with instructions to go to bed and wash thoroughly with soap the next morning. Morning came, breakfast over, but the Doctor had failed to appear. Walton hastened to his room. "Is it you, James?" "Yes." "Come in. I am ruined." (In those days the hair was worn long). There stood the doctor with a mass of dishevelled hair of every shade of color from white to black—like Jacob's cattle—ring-streaked, striped, speckled and spotted. His friend James was so convulsed with laughter at his ludicrous appearance that he could not speak at first; but at last seeing the lugubrious expression of his face, came to his relief by telling his he would have the barber to shave off the hair, and substitute a handsome wig. The Doctor was cheered, the wig put on and he started for home. On his way to Charleston some of his cattle had become tired and he was forced to leave them with a farmer some distance from the city. Reaching the man's house on his return, he said he had come for his cattle. "I have no cattle of yours, Sir," said the farmer. The Doctor tried to convince him of the fact but the farmer said: "You can't fool me. An old white-headed man left some cattle with me, but no such looking buck as you," and he utterly refused to give the cattle up 'til the Doctor of necessity had to take off the wig, and explained the metamorphosis to the satisfaction of the farmer.

Colonel Carson, like a great many of the best class of the citizens of "Auld Lang Syne," was fond of old peach brandy, and would occasionally indulge rather freely in his libations; but instead of pouring out according to the heathen mode on the earth, he poured it in as a solace to human infirmities. When under its influence he wore a kind of turban of red color; at other times and more frequently the turban was white, and he was known to be all right.

THE CONNELLYS (Incomplete, from manuscript)

Forming one of the most extensive families of what was originally Burke County are the descendants of an ancestor, John Connelly, who emigrated to the Colonies from Ireland in 1743 and settled in what was then a part of the original precinct of the Lords Proprietors, Craven County, now Lenoir County. His eldest son (called Little John) (history furnished me by S. E. Connelly of McDowell, taken from a long geneology of the Connellys, kept by his father, John, late of Burke), was a captain in the Revolution and commanded a company in the battle of Kings Mountain. From him descended four sons: William, Allen, George and Joseph. From William descended the Connellys of Caldwell; Henry, Wesly, Alfred, George, Pickens, and Col. Wm. L. Connelly. The last named is the father of the late William and H. A. Connelly. Wm. Connelly, who was the father of Dutch John and Big Bill, as he was called, must have been the brother of Capt. John. Of this, however, I have no information. All of the Connellys of Burke, Caldwell and McDowell have since my earliest . . .

The Corpenings (Incomplete, from manuscript)

With scarce an exception they confide and believe in the honesty of their neighbors. A proof of this came to my surprise, under my personal knowledge and observation on the evening previous to the election. I stayed all night with an intelligent friend of mine, living on his farm near the Upper Fork election ground. In a large room Mr. C., myself and a number of his family slept during the whole night where a number of men were constantly coming and going in and out of the room, sitting by the fireplace and talking in a low tone. After breakfast, sitting alone in the room, a young man, one of Mr. C.'s sons came in and took from the mantle-piece, a large pocketbook, some silver money, and replaced the pocketbook. "Mr. Corpening, sir," I said, "do you keep your pocketbook exposed, lying on your mantle-piece, and persons coming in at all hours of the night?" He replied: "That pocketbook belongs to two of my sons; they keep their money in common. When either makes money they put it in the pocketbook, and each one takes out when he needs it. Our neighbors are honest; they won't steal. I have no locks on my doors. My crib and smokehouse are never locked." What an unpremeditated eulogy pronounced on the South Mountain people! So we see verified the old couplet: "Honor and fame from no condition rise." Act well your part . . . and how true the old adage: "An honest man is the noblest work of God." A great many of these people and their ancestors are of Dutch descent and among the first settlers of more than a century ago. Among these are the Hoffmans, Mulls, Lails, Settlemeyers, Hilbebrands, Carswells, Warlicks and others.

The Estes Family

*(From manuscript, probably published in
Morganton Herald in 1894 — files lost).*

The Estes family, old citizens of Burke descendants of REUBEN ESTES and his wife Delphia Atkins, came from Petersburg, Va., at a very early time to this section of Burke County, and settled on the waters of Johns River, not far from what is known as the Globe (taking the name Globe from the circular form of the surrounding mountains of the Blue Ridge), forming a beautiful valley through which Johns River meanders, celebrated for the alluvial soil, cultivated by prosperous, ambitious farmers. From these two pioneers, Reuben and his wife, have descended one, if not the most numerous of the families of the county, springing from eight children, and giving them alliterative names, the only instance I ever heard of, viz.: Laban, Lou, Lot, Lance, Larken, Lagston, Latta and Lancy. Their children numbered 56 by their marriage with the Webbs, Browns, Gilberts, Coffeys, Moores, Lovings, and Corpenings; and the two and three generations following these, I have no means of estimating the number, which must be very great. I am indebted, besides my knowledge of this large family, to the much-regretted and late worthy citizen, L. J. Estes, the Spainhours and others. I am indebted to Dr. I. M. Spainhour of Caldwell for a very flattering letter in regard to the desultory sketches which I have been writing of the old families, and for an account of the landing of a ship of Bedford from Rotterdam, Sept. 1, 1751(?), emigrants among whom were several with names familiar to Burke, one of whom was Hendrick Corpening, the only one of the name arriving at Philadelphia from 1727 to 1776, the fair presumption being that he was the ancestor of Albert Corpening, who settled in Pennsylvania and moved to Burke in 1803. The same ship carried five of the name of Beck; and one Jacob Hildebrand in the ship St. Andrew, also from Rotterdam. On the same vessel with Jacob came Peter Mull, John Mull and Ia--- Lutz, probably one of those living in this part of N. C., Peter . . ., ancestor of Michael Spainhour and others, Bradshaws, Dr. Dobson, Jo Dobson and Eph Gray.

THE BRADSHAWS OF LOVELADY

Good citizens, plain and unassuming farmers, honest, strict members of the Baptist church, they lived on the Catawba River near the Lovelady Ford. William and Elijah, brothers, I knew when a boy. They kept a seine and had fishing on their own land. The river at that time abounded in fish. In the spring when they were catching shad my father would send me to the Bradshaw's fishery to buy fish, and he previously would save all the old Spanish 12½-cent pieces to pay for the fish, as it was known that the owners would exact that kind of money. Going for the first time I was much interested in the fishing. After they caught quite a number, they divided fish, four of them being interested in the catch. Among the fish they caught there was a very large one that I was anxious to buy. A man by the name of Hicks seized the fish and said he intended to have it. I said: "Not unless you will pay more than I," saying I would give 25 cents for it. "No," said William Bradshaw, "they are all the same price. Our father told us never to take more nor less than a Spanish shilling for a shad, for if we did so we would lose our luck." This closed the dispute,

Hicks getting the fish, twice the size of any other at the same rate. Shad for many years after the Revolution were caught in large numbers in the Catawba River. I heard my father say that when a young man he went to James Locks, who had a fall trap in the river. They made what is called a bush drag, some distance above the trap, then after getting the drag, shouting and pushing it before them to the mounth of the trap, they caught 500 shad; but there are so many obstructions in the river, and particularly one at Rocky Mount, S. C.

(The following pages reproduce certain correspondence between Col. Walton and his wife, and are included for their possible historical value, but chiefly here because of their human commentaries on the hopes and conditions of life at this particularly unfortunate period of Amercian history).

Camp Wyatt, May 2d . 1862

My Dear Wife,

As an opportunity presents by one of my men going home, I write to acknowledge the receipt of the Box brought by Tom McEntire, for which I am much obliged; it remained in Wilmington several days after its arrival before I got it, everything in good order except the Rolls, the loaf bread was very little injured and I have enjoyed toast made from it very much, the Butter is very nice, and a great treat to us who have been so long without. Please give my love to Lauretta and many thanks for the Ham, it came in good for we were out with no prospect of getting any: we occasionally get some milk from a kind Lady living in the Neighborhood.

I believe I mentioned in my last that Henry Mott had joined the company; his Father staid with us on Tuesday night; he is looking better than I ever saw him; he said he thought he would like to be in the army. I like young Mott very much; he and Tom McEntire, Jink and Hugh Tate, will form a Mess. Some 10 or 11 of my men have dysentery but are all recovering. I turned over the Medicine chest to Hugh and he has been attending them since his arrival. The detachment from my company sent to Onslow have not returned, and the General told he yesterday that he would order me and the balance there in a few days. We are expecting Burnside daily and preparations are being made to receive him; two regiments passed down the river to Smithville today. A telegraph line is nearly completed from Fort Fisher to Wilmington which will give direct Telegraphic communication with Goldsboro. It is to be hoped that Burnside will meet with more opposition at this point than the Yankee fleets did at New Bern and New Orleans. I am satisfied that wooden vessels cannot pass the Fort, and think even ironclads will have a hard time of it, if our men fight as they should. I think it probable I may be with you by the 1st of June. Gene French says that by the conscription act the company must reorganize, and I of course cannot hold my position unless I reenlist for the War, and you should know I have made a solemn pledge to you that I would not do so without your assent, and unless you do so, I shall be faithful. My men are very much opposed to my leaving, and it will be a source of regret to me, but there are claims on me at home paramount to every other consideration, not the least among them, after my own dear family, is the duty which I owe my Mother. She has been sadly afflicted in her old age, and my presence may happily soften some of the pangs of her declining years in these times so distressing even to the youthful and robust. I am very much afraid the taking of New Orleans and the coast towns will deprive us of two necessaries of life, Sugar and Salt. Sugar cannot now be bought in Wilmington at less than 24 cts pr. lb. by the barrel. Salt at $6. pr Bushel. If you have any sugar left you will know how to husband it. I would have bought some at this high price but could not get transportation for it. I have no doubt it will be much higher in a few days unless a decisive successful blow is struck by our armies at Corinth and Yorktown, which I hope and believe will be the case. The papers say if Lowell succeeds in leading his Army so as to reinforce Beauregard in time for the Battle of Corinth, and enable him to crush the Northern Army, the fall of New Orleans will be more than compensated.

My health and appetite is very good now and I am gaining flesh. I have heard indirectly from Jink since he went to Onslow — all well; they have had no encounter with the Yankees yet. I met with one of Capt. Hill's company who told me that a gentleman living just across the White Oak river near them had proffered to give them 50 Negroes out of 60 if they would save them from the Yankees. This would be a fine field for a Guerrilla Corps to operate in. I received a letter from your Papa which I was glad to get and am much obliged to him for it. I will answer it shortly. I don't believe I ever thanked you for the nice pants you sent me; they fitted very well, and I keep them for particular occasions. I send by Pearcy some candy for the children. The blocks of wood is a puzzle which I thought Hal would like to work at, when properly put together it forms a ball. I also send Jink's daguerrotype. *If you do not prefer the original I will send you mine instead of coming home.* Give my love to all Friends. Kiss all my darling children and believe me your husband, **devotedly**

T. Geo. Walton

P.S. — I had just closed my letter when your interesting letter, with so much about my dear Children and home was received. I had anticipated a good many of your queries as you will find. I rec'd also a letter from Mr. Roberts on the Sug(?) question; he seems to be rather despond but confidently believe that eventually we will succeed. This series of reverses our arms have met with, and speaks of my seeing sunlight when all is darkness. Until I become satisfied that our cause is bad and God has withdrawn his countenance from us I will not despond but confidently believe that eventually we ewill succeed. This is no time to despair, but on the contrary put forth our whole energy and determine to be annihilated rather than be made serfs — if this feeling only pervaded the bosoms of our whole people (as it does a large majority) the world in arms could never conquer us. The day is not far distant when good news will be heralded to the People of the South, or I shall be sadly disappointed. The Yankees have us at great advantage wherever they can use their Gun Boats, but wherever we have met them inland, with anything like equal numbers, Victory has perched upon our banners.

I send you a quire of paper out of my small store, and will send you stamps whenever you need them.

Good night dear Wife
T. Geo. Walton

(Copy of letter from Col. Walton to his wife, Eliza Murphy Walton)

Camp Wyatt (N. C.)
April 26th, 1862

My Dear Wife:

I received yours of the 20th on the 24th. I enjoyed it very much. I assure you its length was no objection, the first thing I notice when I open your letter is whether any part of the sheet is blank. I have read it three times so you may judge whether I am becoming tired of them. On the contrary I would be miserable if they were not regularly received. Your remark about sharing my room will not soon be forgotten. A portion of my company has been ordered to Onslow. I fretted a good deal on account of it at first, inasmuch as the general would not let me accompany them, thinking, as I did, that it was the post of danger as well as honor; but I have become somewhat reconciled since learning from Capt. Hill that the enemy had withdrawn to New Berne. Jink went, as he has a great love of adventure, and makes a first-rate soldier. He is very popular with the men. Tom McEntire has not reached here yet, and I am uneasy at his delay.

A very exciting scene has just occurred here. Early yesterday morning I received notice that the celebrated Nashville steamboat, which has been so successful in running the blockade, was in sight, having been chased for 12 hours; and couriers were immediately sent to Wilmington for steam and sailing vessels to aid her in crossing the bar of the inlet opposite Fort Fisher. In a short time a number of us mounted and repaired to the beach, and sure enough there lay the model ship, which had so often bid defiance to and outwitted the Yankees, just outside the breakers, calmly waiting the approach of the light draught steamers which were to pilot her through the inlet. Soon they came in sight, and the noble vessel slowly steamed down the beach to meet them.

We galloped along the beach, the surf breaking over our horses' feet, endeavoring to keep pace with her, when within two miles of the mouth of the inlet a shout proclaimed a blockading vessel in sight; and behold in the distance, like a white thunder cloud, every sail set, using every exertion to get within hailing distance, the Yankee came.

The Nashville now steamed along in gallant style. See, she enters the inlet, the guns of the Fort all manned to fire a salute of rejoicing at her safety, when it was discovered that she has ceased to move and is fast aground upon the bar. The guns of the Fort are heavily shotted, the casemates cleaned for action, hundreds of soldiers and officers are on the ramparts of the Fort, and the top of the mound which covers the casemated guns, one second looking to the fast approaching Yankee and the next at the tugboats that are straining their machinery to pull the Nashville over the bar; but in vain their efforts, and all now expect she will be shelled and probably the vessel and valuable cargo lost unless the Yankee can herself be sunk by the fire from the Fort. She (the Yankee) is now so near that the stars and stripes on her flags can be seen; everybody is ordered off the beach, and men voluntarily leave exposed positions, as she suddenly heaves to and turns her broadside to the Fort. I stood on the top of the casemate, and with a glass could count her portholes. She carries 34 heavy guns. After remaining in this position for half an hour, she went off as fast as she had come, as if to give notice to the balance of the blockading fleet of the condition of the Nashville. By working all night, taking off a portion of her cargo, she was finally got off the bar this morning, and is now lying safely in the mouth of the river. There is great rejoicing. I understand her cargo consists of 18,000 Enfield rifles, several tons of powder, and a large quantity of clothing for the soldiers.

The Nashville is a fine vessel and does not fear the Yankee Navy when at sea, being very fast, making 18 or 20 miles an hour. Her commander deserves great credit for his skill and gallantry, as well as performing such good service for the Southern Confederacy.

I will send you Jink's daguerrotype by one of my men, Pearcy, who will be discharged in a few days . . . Mr. Mott's youngest son, Henry, is here and has joined my company. I like him very much. He is very gentlemanly and intelligent, and I think will be an advantageous acquisition to us.

I suppose the conscription will be a bitter pill to some persons in Burke. It seems to be a harsh law, but I am satisfied in the present emergency was a necessary one. The enlistment of many trained soldiers was about to expire, and I have no doubt many regiments would have failed to reorganize under the old law. I am sure the one near us (Iverson's) would not have done so. It would have been a great pity to have lost even it, being the best drilled I have ever seen. We have no sickness in camp, except a few cases of diarrhea (slight).

Tell Tillly Father read her letter with great pleasure, and thanks her very much for it, and hopes it will not be long before I can kiss her for it . . . I am sorry there is no prospect of renting the Walton House. I think if William would exert himself it might be done. It is a pity at a time when there will be such demand for board that so good a house should be lying idle . . . I sold my sorrel mare day before yesterday for $175.00. I was afraid of her eyes and had no use for her. I sold also the black horse. He has never entirely recovered from the distemper and is still poor. I got $147.00 for him. Reeves is doing very well, cooks very well and frequently surprises me by a cup of milk, which he gets from some of his friends — he says honestly.

The mail is about leaving and I must close. Goodbye, sweet wife, until I write again, which will be as soon as I get your answer.

Your devoted husband,
T. Geo. Walton

Give my love to all my dear relatives. T.G.W.

Creek Side Dec. 26th (1861?)

My dear Husband,

I received your letter this evening. I could not help but be disappointed at not hearing from you as you *promised from Statesville* except through a note to Mr. Pearson he sent out to me, but I suppose your motto must be for the present "business before pleasure." I am glad to hear for your sake of your kind treatment upon the way and particularly of your comfortable quarters in Tent and good health. I thought of you much during the sleet and rain upon Christmas; you did not mention it. I think you must have forgotten it. This is the third Christmas we have been separated in 20 years. I felt quite sad. *My good kind* Sister Harriett and William came home with me from Church and staid until night. I am sure it will be a pleasure to know your voice is much missed in the responses. The girls dceorated the Church quite prettily and the musick was quite sweet, particularly to me as I was only a listener.

Mr. Roberts spent last night with us. Wm., Sister H. and myself went to the head of the road to get Cedars for the Church yd. The cars came in without a passenger. Mr. Fisher's mules were going to Salisbury to be sold would not it have been well for you to buy a couple. Julia Happoldt said she saw Less (?) Tate in Salisbury for a few minutes. I heard your men lost some whiskey by accident as you went on, or rather through a mistake of Lieut. Avery's. All of our friends are kind. Papy staid with me the second night after you left and Ma has sent out saying I must come in to see her tomorrow. I know I will feel sad as you have always been there with me. I am doing my best to be cheerful. All the afternoons are sad as the time draws near when you generally came home. I can't bear to think this will last for twelve months but this is an old story and I fear you will weary of my common place letter. Men are not like women; they are taken up with other things and are not so dependent upon their wives for happiness. It seems all a dream to me your getting up and leaving with a company. I can't believe it hardly now — *how could you do it?*

Mr. Roberts says he don't think it was necessary while there were so many young men who could be better spared than you from home; and I wife-like advanced your own reasons for so doing. Don't you believe for a moment I am growing patriotic. I am done with it; I believe it all talk. What do you think will be the effect of England's course? I hope and pray daily a speedy peace for us and a return of my *dear dear* husband to his family. I don't know whether you will read all my scribble but I want you to keep your promises to write. I will live upon your letters and don't stint me too much. Did you forget the change you were to leave at the bank for me or were your funds too low? I don't know whether postage stamps enough. I asked Hugh what to tell "Pappy he says he wants him to come home an Billy Bethel he wants to see him" he is not alone in that. We heard that Mr. James Patton died Saturday night. Mr. Roberts is expecting to hear by the next mail that his Father is dead. I have sayed all I can think of that will interest you and must beg you to write often to your dear wife. All the Children send love to you.

Yours devotedly

E. M. Walton

P.S. — Jimmy says write him as soon as you know when he must start. Also let me know any thing you want me to send you by him that you have forgotten or have found out you need. Don't you throw my letters about where the boys may get them. Tell Willie all are well at home.

(Three letters copied in January 1961 from the manuscript in the *Eliza Murphy Walton Papers* in the Southern Historical Collection at the University of North Carolina Library, Chapel Hill, North Carolina)

(This, the concluding portion of this collection, comprises
so much of the diary of John Murphy Walton as available; no
reason is assignable to its rather abrupt conclusion in December, 1864, but it cannot but be felt by the reader that about
this time, too, ended all but scantest hope for the survival of
the Confederacy which he served).

JOHN WALTON, born Oct. 19, 1844, died Dec. 2, 1872
Enlisted Spring 1863?, 6th Regiment, Co. D, Col. S. McD. Tate

An interesting account of the maneouvers described in this diary
is found in the New Larned History, vol. 10, pp. 8928, et seq., also in
History of the Civil War, 1861-65, by James Ford Rhodes. Some notes
from these books have been placed in the diary as footnotes.

John Walton returned to his home after the surrender on April 9,
1865, having walked a good part of the way, from Petersburg, it is
thought. When his mother came out to greet him he stopped in the
yard at an outhouse and bathed and burned all his clothes before
going in to see his sisters. He was one of 11 children, two of whom
died in early life and two brothers serving in the Confederate Army.

On July 2-4, 1864, Gen. Early engaged the Union forces under
Lew Wallace at Monacacy River and opened the way to Washington.
On July 11-12, as stated by John Walton, the Confederate troops were
within five miles of the Capitol, and fought at Ft. Stephens (Georgia
Avenue near Whittier Street). This was as near as the Confederates
ever got to Washington (now in the city limits). The home of Mr.
Blair spoken of is just over the District line in Maryland. This is the
same Mr. Blair spoken of in history as having "officiously" arranged
a conference between Lincoln and Vice-President Stephens on board
a steamer near Fort Monroe, known as the Hampton Roads Conference. Winston Churchill has recently stated in his history that if the
Confederates had been able to push on down 7th St. to the Capitol
on July 11-12 the end of the war might have been different; but
before they did the Union forces were reinforced.

When the Confederates arrived in Frederick, Md. (see July 9)
there was difficulty in obtaining food, as the farmers drove their
cattle over into Pennsylvania, and the storekeepers shut up shop, not
wishing to accept Confederate money. The principal object of Sheridan's battles and raids August-October 1864 through the Shenandoah
Valley was to prevent the farmers from threshing their wheat and
furnishing provisions to the Confederates.

JOHN MURPHY WALTON'S DIARY

May 17, 1864: En route to Petersburg. Arrived there the night of
the 17th. Stationed at Battery No. 11. Removed to Battery No. 5 on
night of the 19th. Left Petersburg the 25th, marching in the direction
of Richmond. Arrived at Richmond the morning of the 26th. Transported from there to Hanover Junction, continually moving along the
line.

June 4: Twelve miles north of Richmond. Threw up strong breast-works. No general engagement has occurred as yet. We are on the left for the present. Here we had heavy skirmishing. Lieut. Mebane was killed and Capt. McPherson was severely wounded on the 7th. Our regiment suffered a good deal. Ordered to the rear in the evening. Wrote to my dear mother.

Evening of the 9th: The whole corps commenced moving to the right. Marched about 2 miles. Here we bivouaced for the night . . .

June 11: Orders to prepare for Inspection, which will be for tomorrow, Sunday.

Monday, 13th: Commenced moving in the direction of the Valley. Marched 25 miles today. March to be continued this morning. Marched all day. Distance of about 20 miles.

Wednesday, 16th: Marched all day, took the train next morning about 15 miles from Charlottesville. Arrived at Lynchburg at 12 o'clock on the 17th. Yanks about 5 miles from the town. Marched in the evening and commenced throwing up breastworks. Skirmishing has been going on this evening. Enemy has been shelling us. No damage. They made an assault on our right and were repulsed with ease. Left their dead on the field.

June 18: Found the enemy had left their position and were falling back in the direction of Liberty. Arrived in the evening at Liberty. Found the enemy skirmishers in position. Ours attacked and drove them off without any difficulty, killing several, which were left on the field. Lieut. Fleming was wounded. Marched into the town at sundown.

June 20: Marched 17 miles. I am very tired. Heat and dust are very disagreeable.

June 21: Continued to follow the enemy. Marched about 25 miles. The men are very tired. Found enemy had crossed the Gap. They were expected to offer resistance. Our cavalry made a dash at their artillery and wagon trains. Destroyed 20 and captured 10 pieces of artillery, 6 of which they were forced to put down. Camped for the night and drew two days' rations. The mountains look very natural, remind me of home.

Wednesday, June 22, 8 a.m.; Still lying where we bivouaced the first night. It is reported that we will remain here today and rest. I do hope it may be true for we are certainly in need of the rest, though we rested sure enough today. Col. Tate, Dr. Hardy, Brown and myself took a bath, which we enjoyed very much. On our return stopped at Botetout Springs, and drank some sulphur water. There is a Female Seminary near the springs. The General and Officers had a dance there this evening. I went over and looked on. Was not very favorably impressed with the ladies.

June 23: Resumed the march this morning, 3:30 o'clock. Moved in the direction of Buchannon. Arrived there in the evening. Bridge had been burnt. Crossed on planks that were laid on the rafters. Bivouaced.

June 25: Moved at 3 a.m. Arrived at Lexington at 8 a.m. Marched through graveyard with arms reversed. Saw Gen. Jackson's grave, and the Military Institute and the home of Gov. Latcher, which was laid in ruins by the enemy a short time ago. Bridges were burnt. Crossed on plank laid on the rafters. Marched about 18 miles. Arrived at Fairfield at 2 o'clock.

June 26: Resumed the march 3 p.m. Passed through Midway and Smithville. Marched 13 miles. Bivouaced at 12 a.m.

June 27: Moved at 4 a.m. I'm very much pleased with the Valley and community. Find them very hospitable and kind. Have been faring sumptuously for three or four days on butter and milk. Marched 9 miles and bivouaced. Wrote a letter this evening and received one from Pa. Resumed the march June 28 at 3:30 a.m. Arrived at Staunton, took the Valley Pike, passed through Mt. Sidney. Kept the turnpike to the left. Took a road known as Keezle. After marching 11 miles bivouaced at 12 a.m.

June 29: Resumed march at 3:15 a.m. Arrived at Keezletown at nine. Marched 18 miles. Bivouaced at 3 p.m. Still getting butter and milk. The boys have been foraging today. Had apple butter, milk and lightbread.

June 30: Resumed march at 3:15 a.m. Entered turnpike four miles from Newmarket. Arrived at Newmarket at 9 a.m. Marched 16 miles. Bivouaced on branch of Shenandoah, at 1 o'clock p.m. Took a bath this evening which I enjoyed very much. Had a shower of rain. Hope we'll have more as we are very much in need of it.

July 1, 1864: Moved at 4 a.m. Passed through Mt. Jackson to Edenburg. Marched in the direction of Strasburg and bivouaced, distance 18 miles.

July 2: Resumed march. Passed through Strasburg, Middletown and Newtown and bivouaced within 4 miles of Winchester. March 26 miles. Moved at 4:30 a.m. and passed through Winchester to Smithfield.

July 3: Marched 20 miles near Leesburg and bivouaced.

July 4: Resumed march at 4 a.m. Passed near Charlestown, moving in direction of Harper's Ferry. Arrived within 2 miles of the Ferry at 10 a.m. See the flags very distinctly on the heights. Our regiment moved down on the railroad. Detail was made to take the road. Skirmishers were sent out. The enemy are shelling from the heights. Moved back from the railroad after dark and bivouaced.

July 5: Remained quiet and made out payroll and drew two months' wages.

July 6: Still in bivouac. Troops have all crossed the river at Shephardstown. Our brigade has been left here. Moved nearer to the town this morning. Some shelling has been going on from the enemy's batteries this evening.

July 7: Relieved first corps of sharpshooters. Commanded by Sergeant Faucette. They have been shelling us occasionally but doing no damage. Have a vidette post near the river, about half a mile from one of their batteries. Can see very distinctly their line of battle. Received orders to march towards Shephardstown. Moved rapidly all night. Crossed the Potomac below Shephardstown[1], Boonsboro and Middletown and bivouaced after marching 35 miles, in the edge of the town.

July 9: Moved at 2 a.m. Arrived at Frederick City about 9 o'clock. Found the enemy had taken position about 5 miles from town, across the river.

Artillery was put in position and opened on them a heavy fire, which was kept up briskly during the day. In the evening. Gen. Gordon crossed and made the attack, repulsed and routed them completely, and then crossed the Railroad Blockhouse this side where the enemy had left a great deal of plunder. Moved on in the direction they were retreating about a mile. Found they were fleeing in the direction of Baltimore. Moved back near Blockhouse and bivouaced.

July 10: Resumed march this morning[2]. Marched all day in the direction of Washington until 12 o'clock at night, distance of about 26 miles. Resumed march at daylight, July 11. Passed through Rockville and marched about 19 miles by 3 p.m., where we were drawn up in line of battle, five miles from Washington, in the rear of F. P. Blair's house.

July 12: There has been some skirmishing and artillery firing this morning. We were in range of their heavy guns at the forts. Remained until 12 o'clock in the evening and moved in the direction of Rockville. Came to Georgetown Road at dark. We were drawn up in line of battle to prevent any movement on that road by the enemy. Remained until 12 o'clock. Marched all night. (The retreat)

---

(1) Writer afterward told his sister (Florence Walton Pearson) the men crossed wading the stream three abreast, a short man between two taller ones. Writer was a very short man, as was his father, Col. T. Geo. Walton.

(2) See note on Gen. Early on first page.

Wednesday, 13th: Passed through Rockville. Marched until 2 o'clock. Rested until sunset, when march was resumed. Moved slowly all night. Retarded a great deal by the wagon trains.

Thursday, 14th: I feel very tired and sleepy, having marched two successive nights. Arrived at Potomac about 9 o'clock a.m. Crossed at White's Ford. Moved in direction of Leesburg. Bivouaced. Ordered to prepare one day's rations. The enemy threw a few shells inot our regiment from battery on the other side of the river. No damage done. Remained quiet all night.

Friday 15th: Moved across a field into the woods. Col. Tate, Lieut. Brown and myself went and took a bath this evening.

July 16th: Commenced moving in the direction of Leesburg. Passed through that town about 10 o'clock. The enemy made a dash on our wagon trains at 3 p.m. Captured several, most of which were destroyed. We captured a field of their artillery. After marching about 16 miles bivouaced near Snickersville, on mountain. (A range of the Blue Ridge.)

July 17: Moved at 7 a.m. across the Gap. Arrived at Shenandoah and crossed. Marched in the direction of Charlestown. Reported that we will remain in camp several days.

Monday 18: Still in bivouac. Heard the Yanks had made a raid on Morganton. Wrote a letter to Pa and Sis. Moved camp a short distance. Marched this evening about 5 miles and passed through Berryville. Moved in the direction of Shenandoah. Bivouaced about a mile from this town.

July 19: Wrote to Jink this morning. Heard of the death of Aunt Loretta, also of Capt. Blackwell, and that Mr. W. W. Avery had received a very severe wound which caused his death. I am very anxious to get a letter from home and hear the particulars of the raid on Morganton. Marched all night. Arrived at Winchester about daylight on the 20th.

20th: Formed line in rear of works about a mile from Winchester, where we remained until evening. Moved forward. I took command of first corps of sharpshooters. We formed line of battle in the rear of the skirmishers. The enemy charged. We fell back to breastworks in great confusion. Loss slight. Commenced moving at dark. Marched until 12 p.m. Bivouaced near Kearnetown.

July 21: Moved at daybreak. Formed a line of battle in edge of Newtown, where we remained for two hours. Passed through Middletown. Rested a short distance from this town, and marched within 5 miles of Strasburg. Bivouaced about 5 o'clock. Col. Tate, Dr. Bickers, Samuel Brown and myself took a bath.

July 22: Moved in the direction of Strasburg at 4 p.m. Arrived in sight of Strasburg, took a road this side, known as Middle Road. After marching a short distance we turned to the left and formed a line of battle. In the evening my company, B, and K, went on picket, Capt. York commanding, about a mile from the brigade.

July 23: Still on picket. All quiet. Has been some skirmishing about 2 miles off. Relieved in the evening.

Sunday 24: Moved at daylight. Found the enemy near Winchester. Were attacked on the right and repulsed with heavy loss. We moved forward on the left in line of battle, two miles. Arrived at forts beyond town. Found they had retreated in the direction of Harper's Ferry in great confusion, burning ordnance, trains, etc. Bivouaced near Winchester.

Monday 25: Remained quiet today. Rained this morning. Very damp and disagreeable. Wrote and received a letter from home. Moved at 5 p.m. in direction of Martinsburg. Marched about 13 miles and bivouaced, near Darksville.

Tuesday 26: Marched at sunrise. Approached Martinsburg via Darksville. Arrived at 12 o'clock. Found the Yanks had fled. Went into camp and commenced destroying the railroad late in the evening. Continued until 10 o'clock when we returned to camp.

Wednesday 27: Remained in camp all day. Men all washing. Dr. Bickers and myself took a bath in the evening.

Thursday 28: Held an election for the Governor this morning. Vance was elected unanimously. Col. Tate made a short speech. After being cheered by the men the band closed by playing Dixie. Heard good news from the West. Commenced tearing up railroad in the evening. Tore up twice the length of the regiment, and returned to camp. Orders to prepare two days' rations. Wrote a letter to Pa this evening.

Friday 29: Resumed march at daylight. Took Valley Pike. Moved in the direction of Williamsport. Arrived within two or three miles of Williamsport. at 12 a.m. A detachment of Rhodes' division crossed the river and entered the town. We remained in camp until next morning.

Saturday 30: Marched at daybreak in direction of Martinsburg and arrived at daylight.

Sunday 31: Marched rapidly. Arrived at Bunker Hill about 11 o'clock and bivouaced.

Monday, August 1: Reported will remain for several days. Very much disappointed, mail distriubted and didn't get a letter.

Tuesday, August 2: Went and took a bath with Dr. Hardy. Johnston's band came over to headquarters and gave us some splendid music. Orders to prepare for inspection.

Wednesday 3: Inspection at 10 a.m. Took command of three companies and went as far as Gerardtown, acting as a patrol to arrest all citizens and soldiers within the conscript age. Arrested three citizens and six soldiers. On return to camp found regiment on picket. Remained until morning. Marched at 3:30 a.m. in direction of Williamsport. Bivouaced near Hedgeville.

Friday 5 (1): Resumed march at 5 a.m. Crossed the Potomac at Williamsport. Visited Col. Avery's grave. Felt very sad. Marched until about two. Bivouaced near St. James College. Received two letters this evening. Very gratifying.

Saturday 6: Returned to Williamsport, crossed the river. Marched about 18 miles and bivouaced about five miles from Martinsburg.

August 7: Moved at sunup. Marched until 12 a.m. when we arrived at former camp at Bunker Hill. Regiment went on picket.

August 8: Relieved by 57th Regiment. Returned to camp. Took a bath with Drs. Tate and Bickers.

August 9: Moved in the direction of Winchester. Arrived on the Romney Road in the evening, when we formed a line of battle. Brigade of cavalry has gone to the front.

Wed., Aug. 10: Remained quiet. Moved down on Pike Road. Moved within about half a mile of Winchester. Moved on . . . Road a short distance from Winchester where we bivouaced.

August 11: Moved a short distance. Formed a line of battle. Some Skirmishing and cannonading for a short time. Commenced moving to the right in the direction of Newtown. Arrived at . . . Rested for the night in line of battle.

August 12: Moved at 3 a.m. in the direction of Strasburg. Bivouaced near Strasburg.

August 13: Commenced throwing up breastworks. Worked all day. Moved out to the front of the town and remained all day.

August 15: Took command of two companies of sharpshooters. Moved out to the front in the evening and returned at sundown to camp. Relieved by the first corps.

August 16: Rained. Had preaching this morning. Col. Godwin appointed Brigadier. Went up with brigade and called on him for a few minutes speech. Said a few words and Major York also spoke.

Moved in the direction of Winchester. Formed a line of battle, two or three miles from Winchester. Heavy skirmishing. Yanks were routed. Moved back half a mile to piece of woods.

(1) On this day Farragut won the Battle of Mobile Bay.

August 18: Passed through Winchester. Moved down on the pike and bivouaced near the old battleground of the 20th (of July).

August 19: Moved in the direction of Bunker Hill.

August 20: Moved in the direction of Smithfield. Found the enemy had fallen back in the direction of Bunker Hill. Rained very hard. Went foraging with Mr. Brown this evening. Got corn, and milk and apples. Marched at sunrise in the direction of Charlestown. Formed line of battle within four miles of Charlestown. Heavy skirmishing all day. Leathres was mortally wounded.

August 22: Moved as far as Charlestown. Found the Yankees had fallen back. Returned to their camp a few miles from town. Brigade was ordered out. Reconnoitered a mile below town and returned. I remained with the cooking detail as I was unwell.

August 23: Remained quiet today. Went with Adjutant and took a bath this evening.

August 24: Moved down below Charlestown on the right. Formed a line of battle, where we remained until next morning of the 25th. Moved in the direction of Shepardstown. Some fighting in front of us all day between infantry and cavalry. Bivouaced two miles from town.

August 26: Remained quiet until 2 p.m. Marched in the direction of Smithfield. Arrived at dusk. Bivouaced.

August 27: Marched at 1 o'clock in the direction of Bunker Hill. Arrived at old camp about 5 p.m. Wrote a letter this morning to Ma.

August 28: Wrote a letter this morning to Jink. On picket about three miles from camp on the Smithfield road. The enemy's cavalry advanced this evening. Had some severe fighting with our cavalry. Ours fell back this side of the creek. Formed a thin line of battle near us at sundown. Everything quiet in front.

August 29: The enemy advanced this morning. Skirmished with ours. Driving them back. Division moves out. We form a line of battle Throw out skirmishers and advance. The Yanks fell back. Follow them a short distance from Smithfield in line of battle. Turn to camp at Bunker Hill.

August 30: Brigade returned to the picket post. Left camp at daylight. Went on picket with company on left hand road. Got a splendid supper. Cavalry crossed the Opegan River in the evening. Have some skirmishing. Returned to camp at dark.

August 31: Remained in camp. Everything seems quiet today. Drew four months' wages from Capt. McNeely this evening.

Sept. 1: Wrote a letter to Ma. I am unwell today. Suffering from dysentery.

Sept. 2: Marched in the direction of Winchester. Rode in the ambulance. Encamped about four miles from Winchester.

Sept. 3: Regiment went on picket in the evening. Received a letter from Ma. Kenshaws attacked the enemy near Berryville. Carried off a portion of their line.

Sept. 4: Moved in the direction of Berryville, arriving within a short distance of town. Form a line of battle to the left of the pike. Take command of first corps. Have some skirmish at short range. Find the enemy position. Relieved at dark by Companies B and K. Find brigade had moved and encamped to the left of the pike in a field to guard wagon train.

Sept. 5: Had a wet and disagreeable night. Returned to the front. Remained until evening and commenced falling back. Have rain. Encamped near old camp near Winchester. Sleeping in an old house.

Sept. 6: Remained quiet today. Continues to rain. Disagreeable.

Sept. 7: Wrote a letter to my dear mother this morning. Regiment goes on picket in the evening to support the 21st. Received distressing news from Atlanta [1].

Sept. 9: Wrote . . . Orders to prepare camping ground, and prepare tents properly.

Sept. 10: Marched in direction of Bunker Hill. Arrived in the evening at old camp.

Sept. 11: Return to camp near Winchester. Commenced making out muster and payrolls.

Sept. 12: Move at 12 o'clock in direction of Charlestown. Halt near Jordan's Springs. Find enemy in sight across the Oppenquan. Having an artillery drill. Returned to camp. Regiment remained on picket. Still have wet disagreeable weather.

Sept. 14: Relieved in the evening by the 57th Regiment.

Sept. 15: Moved in direction of Winchester. Camped near. The town in sight. We commenced the muster rolls. Complete rolls on the 16th. Received letter from home. Visit Winchester at night. The 17th relieves the 21st on picket.

Sept. 17: Relieved the 21st on picket.

Sept. 18th: Relieved by 57th. Returned to camp. Attenoded preaching by Dr. Lacy.

---

(1) Atlanta was captured by Sherman on Sept. 3.

Sept. 19 (1): Enemy attacks Winchester at dawn of day. Severe fighting all day. We were beaten back in the evening, and commenced to retreat near sundown in the direction of Strasburg. Enemy have charged us twice and were repulsed with ease. Bivouaced near Newtown.

Sept. 20: Resumed retreat at daybreak. Arrived at breastworks near Strasburg.

Sept. 21: Remained quiet. Received a letter from Sis. Heavy skirmishing in front. Later in the evening Sharpshooters compelled to fall back a short distance.

Sept. 22: Took command of first company. Enemy advanced and we rere compelled to fall back. In the evening they assaulted on the extreme left. Portion of them getting into our rear. That produced a great panic and everything commenced fleeing in the greatest confusion, leaving the most of our artillery. After running two miles we succeeded in rallying the men. Many of the men went to the mountains. Fell back to Mt. Jackson that night.

Sept. 23: Cavalry advanced and compelled us to fall back a short distance. Our regiment sent out to support them. Major York was wounded. Capt. Gilmore took command.

Sept. 24: Enemy advanced and we retreat in line of battle. Shell us furiously all day. At sundown we form a line of battle near Keezletown. Made breastworks of rails. At nine o'clock we resumed retreat. Took Keezletown road and marched until 12 o'clock. Rested until morning.

Sept. 25: Continued to retreat. Crossed the river near Fort Republic and camped near the Gap.

Sept. 26: Moved out to support the cavalry. Ambuscaded. Skirmishing most of the day. Returned to camp at dark. Col. Tate returned.

Sept. 27: Moved to the front and crossed the river. Reconnoitered about two miles. Some skirmishing.

Sept. 28: Made a hard march today. Arrived near Waynesboro in the evening. Found the enemy's cavalry near the town. Skirmished with it until late at night. Had them almost surrounded at one time. Regiment sent out on picket on the Staunton Pike.

Sept. 29: Relieved in the evening by regiment from Johnston's brigade. Returned to brigade and encamped about a mile from Waynesboro. Orders to move in the morning.

---

(1) In history this is called the Battle of Winchester, also the Battle of Opequan Creek. The Union Army with three times as many men captured 2,500 Confederates. Union forces in front of Berryville.

Sept. 30: Orders countermanded. Wrote to Ma. Remained quiet today.

Oct. 1: Marched in the direction of Mt. Sidney. Rained hard. Very disagreeable. Encampel near the town.

Oct. 2: Wrote to Sis. Rain in the evening. Relieved the 21st on picket. Relieved by the 49th Virginia in the evening. Heard cheering news from Richmond.

Oct. 5: Remained quiet. Attended preaching in the evening by Dr. Reid.

Oct. 6: Marched in the direction of Winchester via Harrisburg. Encamped about a mile from it to right of pike.

Oct. 7: Resumed march at sunup. Arrived at Newmarket about 4 p.m. and camped to the left and rear of town.

Oct. 8: Remained quiet. Capt. McPherson returned.

Oct. 9: Had inspection at 12 a.m. Moved out at sundown near Gordon's Camp. Formed line of battle and remained until after dark. Returned to camp. Very cold and disagreeable. Frost last night.

Oct. 10: Remained quiet and wrote to Jink. Had dress parade. Ordered to have two drills daily.

Oct. 11: Commenced drilling today. Received and answered letter home. Orders to prepare two days' rations.

Oct. 12: Marched in the direction of Strasburg. Camped beyond Edenburg.

Oct. 13: Resumed march. Arrived near Fisher's Hill at 12 a.m., where we rested two hours. Moved beyond Fisher's Hill. Took middle road and moved up it about a mile. Formed line of battle in a field Remained until dark and returned near breastworks at Fisher's Hill and camped.

Oct. 14: Moved out from the camp a short distance. Remained until dark and returned.

Oct. 15: Cold and windy.

Oct. 16: Right wing relieved in the evening, in charge of Capt. McPherson.

Oct. 17: Moved at sunup in the direction of Middle Road. Halted about a mile from camp where we remained a short time. Went on picket at sundown with Companies B and K.

Oct. 18: Returned to camp at dark. Marched all night around the Massanutten Mountains. Very rough road.

Oct. 19[1]: Just at daybreak. Attacked the enemy on the left flank, completely surprising and routing them, driving them near Middletown. Davis was wounded early in the engagement. Col. Tate then took command of the brigade. Late in the evening Col. Tate's extreme left was broken and everything commenced falling back in the greatest confusion. Lost all the artillery we had captured and a great many wagons and ambulances also. Col. Tate was wounded in the retreat. Capt. Beale took command of the brigade. We marched all night.

Oct. 20: Marched all day. Arrived at old camp back at Newmarket. Most of the regiment are missing, though they are coming in hourly.

Oct. 21: Had division inspection this evening. Gen. Pegram lectured the officers of the brigade.

Oct. 22: Remained quiet. Acting Adjutant of the regiment. Made out field returns.

Oct. 23: Remained quiet. Received and wrote a letter yesterday.

Oct. 24: Commenced drilling. Received and wrote a letter home.

Oct. 25: Had coat and vest cut out to be made by Saturday. Visited Newmarket.

Oct. 26: Remained quiet.

Oct. 27: Remained quiet.

Oct. 28: Moved camp.

Oct. 29: Brigade inspection.

Oct. 30: Remained quiet.

Oct. 31: Remained quiet. Very cold and clear.

Nov. 1: Alex started home. Had battalion drill.

Nov. 2: Cloudy and showers most of the day.

Nov. 3: Cold and cloudy. No drill.

Nov. 4: Damp and disagreeable. Rain part of the day.

---

(1) On this day Sheridan having spent the night at Winchester on his return from Washington, awoke to the sound of firing and made his famous ride, rallying his men after defeat. Soon after this Northern victory Southern soldiers were withdrawn to the defense of Petersburg and made no more victories in the North.

Nov. 5: No drill. Men washing. Drew shoes, blankets, etc.

Nov. 6 and 7: Made out muster rolls.

Nov. 7: Received letter from home. Weather continued to be cloudy.

Nov. 8[1]: Wrote a letter. Had division inspection. Orders to move at daylight.

Nov. 10: Marched in the direction of Winchester.

Nov. 11: Marched at daylight. Arrived at Newtown in the evening. Formed a line of battle.

Nov. 12: Remained quiet. Some skirmishing. Returned to Fisher's Hill.

Nov. 13: Marched at sunup and camped near Edenburg.

Nov. 14: Marched at daylight. Snow and very cold. Arrived at old camp near New Market, about 9 o'clock.

Nov. 15: Remained quiet. Had inspection.

Nov. 16: Moved camp nine miles nearer Strasburg.

Nov. 17: Commenced putting up a chimney. Rain all day. Letter from home.

Nov. 19: Snowed this morning. Had dreadful rain in the evening. Rations are short.

Nov. 20: Cloudy and damp. Rain this evening.

Nov. 21: Continues to rain. Disappointed not getting a letter today.

Nov. 21: At last cleared off. Disappointed not getting letter by the mail today. Capt. Bickers and Capt. McPherson went foraigng today. Returned with turkeys.

Nov. 23: Received and wrote letters. Had drill this evening. The weather is exceedingly cold.

Nov. 24: Wrote Jink. Camp life is very monotonous. Men working on their quarters. Making chimney. Had turkey for dinner.

Nov. 26: Weather very cold.

Nov. 27: Had inspection.

Nov. 28: Regimental inspection.

(1) Lincoln was re-elected Nov. 8, 1864.

Nov. 29: Battalion drill.

Nov. 30: Drill. Orders to have company inspection every morning

Dec. 1: Nothing of interest occurred today.

Dec. 2: Very dull. Battalion drill.

Dec. 3: Baggage arrived. Found my things all safe.

Dec. 4: Received two letters and wrote one.

Dec. 5: Regimental inspection.

Dec. 6: Received orders very suddenly to be in readiness to move. Marched at 11 a.m. in the direction of Staunton. Moved rapidly all day. Encamped near Mt. Sidney.

Dec. 7: Marched at 8 a.m. to Waynesboro, six miles from Staunton. Arrived at old camp Waynesboro at sundown.

Dec. 8: Remained quiet all day. Took train at dark for Richmond. Very cold and disagreeable.

Dec. 9: Arrived at Richmond about 12 o'clock. Marched through the town and took Petersburg train. Arrived near Petersburg late in the evening. Marched in front to Works and occupy Lane's quarters.

Dec. 10: Ground covered with snow. Moved to the right about 10 miles in the direction of Stony Creek where we formed a line of battle. Skirmishers moved forward half a mile and returned. We then moved rapidly back to camp. Received a letter from Cousin Lola.

Dec. 11: Regiment and portion of 54th went on picket. Col. Tate returned from home. Brought me a letter and some underclothes.

Dec. 12: Relieved by portion of Pegram's old brigade.

Dec. 13: Moved in the evening. I remained and saw Jink and all my acquaintances in Lane's brigade. Stayed all night with Jink.

Dec. 14: Found the regiment about seven miles from Petersburg on the extreme right in a very pretty place in Gen. Hampton's old camp.

Dec. 15: Commenced putting up winter quarters. Col. Tate and myself are going to stay together. Capt. McPherson and Lieut. Brown have completed their quarters.

Dec. 16: Wrote a letter and superintended putting up shanties.

Dec. 17: Had brigade inspection. Wrote a letter to Cousin Lola.

Dec. 18: Nothing important occurred today. Heard a salute by the enemy of a hundred guns.

Dec. 19: Col. Tate took command of the regiment. Men are policing camp.

Dec. 20: Nothing of importance today.

Dec. 21: Completed quarters.

Dec. 22: Men leaving for home. Those who have furloughs. Wrote a letter and sent it by Joe Brown.

Dec. 23: Capt. McPherson received a furlough though he doesn't intend leaving for several days. Col. Tate is sick and McPherson is in command.

Dec. 24: Nothing of importance today. Mail trains are pressed transporting troops to Washington.

Dec. 25: Clothes are being issued by the regiment. Jink and Willoughby came to see us and stayed all night. Had eggnog.

Dec. 26: Cloudy and disagreeable. Orders to have company and brigade drill daily. Had parade ground cleaned off. Stayed with Dr. Tate all night.

Dec. 28: Brigade inspection. Orders from Gen. Lee. There will be no more furloughs granted for the present.

Wartime Prices (1)

For boy from Morganton to Salisbury	$ 10.00
From Salisbury to Goldsboro	12.50
Supper at Goldsboro	10.00
Raleigh	6.00
Account book	15.00
Cash at Tarboro	10.00
Newspapers	1.00
Paid Alex Allen	20.00
Contributed to B.	10.00
Gave to C.	
Milk	11.00
Mending hat	1.00
Cider	10.00
Soda	18.00
Adjutant Mebane	18.00
Gave Alex	5.00
Gold pen	15.00
Settled with mess	23.00

(1 — At one time during the war 10-penny nails were used in N. C. as the equivalent of five cents in money. Mrs. Jeff Davis reports in her diary that in 1864 the price of a turkey was $60, flour $300 per barrel, and in July shoes 159 dollars a pair in Richmond. A dollar in gold then brought $22 in Confederate money.)

Smoking tobacco	3.00
Apples	6.00
Lieut. Brown	15.00
Brandy	5.00
Bread and chestnuts	3.00
Washing	10.00
Collars and cravat	20.00
Barber at Raleigh	6.00
Cakes	1.00
Breakfast at High Point	3.00
Clothes and shirts	80.00
Lodging at Salisbury	5.00
Bought 3 doz. eggs	15.00
Notebook	5.00
Brandy	10.00
Commissary bill	7.25
Paper and envelopes	10.00
Paid Quartermaster for pants	14.00
Paid A. Tilley mess account	10.00
Portfolio	5.00
Brandy	25.00
Making coat and vest	121.00
Pressing hat	4.00
Gave Alex Allen	100.00

Index to Sketches of the Pioneers of Burke County, N.C. History

www.ingramcontent.com/pod-product-compliance
Lightning Source LLC
Chambersburg PA
CBHW021837020426
42334CB00014B/673